'*Meeting God in John* offers a masterclass Bible Study, a deeply moving devotional meditation, and a rich group experience all focused on encounter with Jesus. David Ford's wonder at the extraordinary love of God for us revealed through John's Gospel is palpable, beautiful and contagious. An amazing journey into the heart of God led by an extraordinarily inspiring guide.'
Professor Paul S. Williams, Chief Executive, Bible Society

I0080258

David F. Ford OBE is Regius Professor of Divinity Emeritus at the University of Cambridge, England, and a Fellow of Selwyn College. His publications include *The Gospel of John: A Theological Commentary*; *Glorification and the Life of Faith* (with Ashley Cocksworth); *A Kind of Upside-Downness: Learning Disabilities and Transformational Community* (with Deborah Hardy Ford and Ian Randall); *Theology: A Very Short Introduction*; *The Future of Christian Theology*; *Christian Wisdom: Desiring God and Learning in Love*; *Living in Praise – Worshipping and Knowing God* (with Daniel W. Hardy); and *Meaning and Truth in 2 Corinthians* (with Frances M. Young).

He chairs the trustees of Lyn's House, Cambridge (a L'Arche-inspired community of hospitality and friendship for those with and without learning disabilities, founded by his wife Deborah and others). He co-chairs the Rose Castle Foundation, a centre for reconciliation, interfaith engagement, religious literacy, and conservation, and the UK hub for interfaith Scriptural Reasoning and Christian Biblical Reasoning, based in Rose Castle in Cumbria, UK.

He lived in inner city Birmingham for fifteen years, for five of which he was Church Warden in his parish church. He has been awarded the Coventry International Prize for Peace and Reconciliation, and honorary degrees by universities in Ireland, England, Scotland and India.

'An excellent companion to encountering God in the person of Jesus Christ as revealed to us in John's "paschal" Gospel. Whether used in a group or individually, in the journey through Lent to Easter and beyond or at any time of the year, this volume will help uncover the depths of this profound Gospel, enriching each reader.'
John Behr, Regius Professor of Humanity, University of Aberdeen

'David Ford's excellent commentary on the Gospel of John is one of my favourites, so to hear that he's produced an accompanying devotional thrills me. Meaty, thought-provoking and hugely discussable, this is a resource for Lent and beyond. Through it you'll meet Jesus, and your faith will be strengthened.'
Amy Boucher Pye, spiritual director and author of *7 Ways to Pray*

'With this utterly lucid study, one of the very best contemporary theologians emulates the simplicity, the depth and, equally, the loving care for readers who wish to follow Jesus that he discovers in John's Gospel. Ford's brilliant close reading of the Greek text enables those with different levels of expertise to plumb the depths and follow the flow of this drama of desire, growing trust and formation in a community of love.'
Ellen F. Davis, Amos Ragan Kearns Professor of Bible and Practical Theology, Duke Divinity School, North Carolina

'In the Eastern Orthodox tradition it is sometimes said that theologians are people who have been taught by God. In this remarkable study resource an outstanding scholar and theologian distils, in accessible form, not only a lifetime's reflection and scholarship on the Gospel of John, but also the fruit of a lifetime's discipleship and attentiveness to the needs of Christian community. He invites us into a Jesus-inspired "drama of desire" for deep meaning and deep love, and offers a personal spirituality that lets God speak to us today through this magnificent Gospel. The result is a unique way into

the promise and fulfilment of "deep, lasting, abundant life" in Jesus Christ.'
John McDowell, Church of Ireland Archbishop of Armagh; Eamon Martin, Roman Catholic Archbishop of Armagh

'David Ford has a deep and pervasive enthusiasm for John's Gospel and has devoted a considerable portion of his life as a teacher and theologian to exploring and expounding its riches. Here is a summary of his wisdom in a book of manageable length for the ordinary reader, to be used in Lent and over Passiontide and beyond.'
Janet Morley, author of *The Heart's Time* and *Love Set you Going*

'David Ford reminds us that in the overwhelming superabundance of the Gospel of John we meet Jesus and are invited to trust and love him for ourselves. Writing in accessible style for individual devotion and group reflection, David encourages us to become habitual readers of the Gospel of John and shows us that there is always more to find and be surprised by in it. I commend David's helpful book to those eager to grow in their Christian faith through the study of John's Gospel.'
Michael Volland, Bishop of Birmingham

'Ford's years of scholarship, prayer, meditation and shared reading of the Gospel of John have been distilled with clarity and depth in this book that draws us into encounter with God. Jesus is at the heart of every page of the Gospel, because this is how we come to know God, in God's self-giving love in Jesus. As we get to know Jesus, we also get to know ourselves, our search for ourselves, our desires, our longing for "home", all revealed and then answered with the overflowing generosity of God's presence with us and for us.'
Jane Williams, McDonald Professor in Chrisitan Theology, St Mellitus College, London

MEETING GOD IN JOHN

A Companion for Lent, Holy Week,
Easter and Beyond

David F. Ford

First published in Great Britain in 2025

SPCK

Part of the SPCK Group, Studio 101, The Record Hall, 16–16A Baldwin's Gardens, London
EC1N 7RJ
https://spckpublishing.co.uk

Text copyright © David F. Ford 2025
This edition copyright © Society for Promoting Christian Knowledge 2025

Author has asserted his right under the Copyright, Designs and Patents Act, 1988, to be
identified as Author of this work.

All rights reserved. No part of this book may be reproduced or transmitted
in any form or by any means, electronic or mechanical, including photocopying,
recording, or by any information storage and retrieval system, without
permission in writing from the publisher.

Unless otherwise noted, Scripture quotations are taken from the New Revised Standard
Version of the Bible, Anglicized Edition, copyright © 1989, 1995 by the Division of
Christian Education of the National Council of the Churches of Christ in the USA.
Used by permission. All rights reserved.

Scripture quotations marked NLT are taken from the Holy Bible, New Living Translation,
copyright © 1996. Used by permission of Tyndale House Publishers, Inc., Carol Stream,
Illinois 60189, USA. All rights reserved.

EU GPSR Authorised Representative
LOGOS EUROPE, 9 rue Nicolas Poussin, 17000, La Rochelle, France
Email: Contact@logoseurope.eu

British Library Cataloguing-in-Publication Data
A catalogue record for this book is available from the British Library

ISBN 978-0-28108-963-5
eBook ISBN 978-0-28108-964-2

10 9 8 7 6 5 4 3 2 1

Typeset by Manila Typesetting Company
First printed in Great Britain by Clays Limited

eBook by Manila Typesetting Company
Produced on paper from sustainable sources

This work is dedicated to

the Church of Ireland

and

the Church of England

in gratitude for the many ways I have met with God in those,
my two Church homes.

And also to

my grandchildren, Solomon, Azalea, Josiah and Pascoe.

Contents

Part 3

THE ONGOING DRAMA: JESUS HAPPENING IN THE TWENTY-FIRST CENTURY

Foreword

Being David Ford's vicar has been one of the great joys – and challenges – of my life. In a brief lull between completing his commentary on John's Gospel and writing the book you are holding, David persuaded me to rewrite the lectionary to give John his own year. We embarked on a quest to 'marinate' our congregation – people of every socio-economic background and level of education – in this extraordinary Gospel, which, as David notes in his introduction, rewards both beginner and expert alike.

Inclusion is only one aspect of the unity that John's Gospel prays for and impresses upon its readers. In its simple vocabulary and recurring themes, beginners find confidence; experts find challenge. David Ford's 'Lent plus' study takes us through many of these themes, looping around the Gospel and showing how they unfold. This is, in fact, how we preached throughout the year – revisiting passages, creating a circular energy that swept our congregation into familiarity with Johannine concepts: 'abide', 'home', 'life', 'truth' and others. Through preaching, café church activities, study breakfasts and tea with celebrity guest speakers, in Lent groups, home groups and through 'Johannine music' that set texts to song, we sought to meet God in John's Gospel. A diverse group of about a dozen people at every stage of faith and knowledge worked through drafts of the first five chapters of this book over five sessions. We appreciated the writer's enthusiasm, the depth of his thought and the probing questions supplied by Revd Canon Amiel Osmaston at the end of each chapter. You will too.

Our year in John's Gospel proved truly extraordinary, as the church grew increasingly able to 'know and trust' Jesus. We also experienced significant growth in numbers – perhaps because the year's sharp focus and energy drew newcomers in. In line with John's emphasis, we constantly focused on love, unity and forming community – such vital imperatives for our time.

John's Gospel speaks directly to the hungers of our age, perhaps more clearly than any other part of the Bible.

I wholeheartedly commend any encounter with this Gospel to you, but especially this one: *Meeting God in John* by Professor David Ford, born of both profound scholarship and joyfully abundant faith.

Revd Dr Karin Voth Harman
Vicar of St Andrew's Parish Church, Cherry Hinton
April 2025

Preface

This book has been a long time in the making – the original contract for it was signed in 2014. Yet it actually came together in its present form as a 'Lent plus' book in June 2023 during a week of intensive engagements and conversations centred on the Gospel of John.

Before that week, a twenty-year project had resulted in the publication in December 2021 of *The Gospel of John: A Theological Commentary*. That long immersion in one of the most important Christian texts has been the most profound experience of my life. Key people and events that fed into the work during those two decades are described in the epilogue of the commentary. But one event in 2015 that is only hinted at there was especially important for this book.

By 2015, I had been working on the John commentary for fifteen years and had written a good deal. Early in that year, I delivered eight Bampton Lectures in Oxford University on 'Daring Spirit: John's Gospel Now'. That involved bringing together years of academic study, research and teaching and also trying, as the title suggests, to open up the importance of John's Gospel for the twenty-first century. The ideal was to combine academic scholarship, interpretation, theology, spirituality and relevance to our time. Given the setting of the lectures, it was inevitable that there was more emphasis on the academic side.

Then, in the autumn of 2015, I retired from my post in Cambridge University and sat down to complete the commentary on John. I reread everything I had written in the previous fifteen years and very reluctantly realised that it simply would not do. It was a crisis. The commentary was meant to be sure-footed academically but primarily aimed at readers beyond the academy. Yet, as I read what I had written so far, it seemed to me to be falling between stools. On the one hand it was aiming at ordinary, non-academic readers, but on the other hand it was carrying on academic discussions and disputes, was heavy with footnotes and did not flow. It felt bogged down in a worthy form, the verse-by-verse commentary – examples of which were piled up in my study. So I scrapped everything I had written and started afresh.

I experimented with a new commentary style and structure. I tried it out on my wife Deborah, a priest and psychotherapist, and on my friend Micheal O'Siadhail, a poet. When they both judged that what I was producing more or less worked, I continued in that mode. It follows John's flow chapter by chapter (though not verse by verse), limits endnotes, tries to be accessible to non-academics (while ringing true with at least some academics), offers as much spirituality as theology and seeks to distil (often in short, italicised sentences) John's wisdom for today. Above all, it tries to communicate the reality of who Jesus is and what following him means today.

So, from that fresh start, the commentary was actually written between 2015 and 2021. But, having signed the contract for this book in 2014, *Meeting God in John* was always in view. The commentary needed a companion aimed at entering deeply into the Gospel of John in the church through group and individual study, which could resource preaching, teaching and living in the twenty-first century. By mid-2023, I had accumulated a mass of notes and a variety of possible shapes for the book. Yet I had slowly realised that there was a massive problem: *Meeting God in John* was meant to be a Lent Book, but John's Gospel could not be fitted into Lent!

Every attempt I made to do justice to John in five sessions suitable for the usual Lent Group pattern resulted in failure. Partly, this is because John, as I read it, is a carefully crafted Gospel that, like the tunic of Jesus, is 'seamless, woven in one piece' (John 19:23) and needs to be understood as a whole, in line with its stated purpose of enabling readers to come to trust who Jesus is and then let that relationship shape their lives (20:30–31). Also, however, it is for the obvious reason that John not only deals with the concern in Lent to prepare for the climactic events of the Last Supper and the suffering, crucifixion and resurrection of Jesus; John also has, of all the Gospels, the fullest account of the events following the resurrection of Jesus, and, in the Farewell Discourses (John 13 – 17), the fullest guidance for the ongoing drama of discipleship in the Christian community. Squeezing all this into Lent seemed impossible. This extraordinary text cries out to be studied both in Lent and after Easter, seamlessly.

A solution came through that unusual week in mid-June 2023 when I was immersed in the Gospel of John. The week included a day at High Leigh Conference Centre studying John with a group of Nigerian Christians; time with the Community of St Anselm in Lambeth Palace (an international group of young Christians from various Christian churches who were completing a 'year in God's time' focused on prayer, study and service), also centred on John; a morning with the men and women, from the Church of England and other churches, who are Canons of Ely Cathedral, studying and discussing John together; an inspiring session given by Jeremy Begbie on Bach's *St John Passion* in my own parish, St Andrew's Church, Cherry Hinton, as part of our 'Year of John'; and a day on John in Stowmarket with around one hundred clergy and lay ministers from the Diocese of St Edmundsbury and Ipswich, at which I collected a card from each with their insights into the Gospel.

The week's climax came in an intensive conversation with Revd Canon Amiel Osmaston, a close friend of my wife and myself who was staying with us. She had led theological education in the Diocese of Carlisle and was experienced with Lent groups. As we wrestled with the dilemma of how to fit John into Lent, she came up with what immediately seemed the obvious solution: of course, I should make it a 'Lent plus' book.

So, as that John-soaked week indicates and as the acknowledgements expand on further, this book, like the commentary, has been nourished by innumerable engagements with a wide range of people and groups. It has been very much a shared process. That seems appropriate for this Gospel. Most scholars see the Gospel of John as being written over many years with diverse elements brought together – eyewitness testimony, a variety of written testimonies to Jesus, experience of living through the ups and downs of an early Christian community and probably some co-authorship. It is a delight to be able to share this fresh attempt to distil from that Gospel – and from encounters with so many people both in person and in print – some core essentials for Christian understanding and practice in the twenty-first century and some ways to go deeper and deeper into the reality to which this extraordinarily rich scripture testifies.

Acknowledgements

Reading, rereading and discussing the Gospel of John with other people has been one of the most fascinating, illuminating and inspiring activities in my life. The debts of gratitude for all the insights, testimonies, questions, arguments, surprises and challenges I have received are incalculable.

One especially intensive period of reading and conversation was during the twenty years between late 2000 and 2021 when I was working on *The Gospel of John: A Theological Commentary*. For the commentary's acknowledgements, I tried to remember and name the dozens of groups and scores of people who had helped to shape the book – family and friends; students and academic colleagues; fellow Christians in many churches and countries; members of other religious traditions, especially Jews, Muslims and Hindus; people working in a range of spheres including business, politics, civil service, medicine, media, education, law, prisons, interreligious engagement and peacebuilding; and various others. I remain grateful to all of them.

Since the publication of the commentary, the fruitfulness and inspiration of John's Gospel has continued, and it shows no signs of diminishing – indeed, rather the opposite. Many of those acknowledged in the commentary have also (some without realising it) fed into this book, written since the commentary's publication. They include Nick Adams, Mother Anne, Barbara Bennett, Georgette Bennett, Richard Bauckham, James Broad, Rob and Joanna Brown, Anna Caffell, Ashley Cocksworth, Ken Costa, Margaret Daly-Denton, Ellen Davis, Lejla Demiri, Beth Dodd, Alan Ford, Annie, Derek and Claire Ford, Jason Fout, Ben Fulford, Joseph Galgalo, Judith Gardom, Loraine Gelsthorpe, Sister Gemma C. J., Nigel Genders,

Acknowledgements

Julie Gittoes, Alon Goshen-Gottstein, Matthias Grebe, Tom and Heather Greggs, Isabelle Hamley, Perrin Hardy, Annie and Alan Hargrave, Richard Harman, Mike Higton, Peter and Catherine Ievins, Carole Irwin, Tim Jenkins, Anderson Jeremiah, Greg Jones, Steve Kepnes, Daniel King, Graham Kings, Dominic Krautter, Patrick Leckie, Robbie Leigh, Georgia and Owen May, Peter McDonald, Dominic McMullen, William McVey, Vittorio Montemaggi, Rachel Muers, Paul Murray, Aref Nayed, Dave Nelson, Ben Quash, Madeleine O'Callaghan, Peter Ochs, Janette Pearson, Alex Radford, Ian and Janice Randall, Krish Raval, Chloe Reddaway, Miikka Ruokanen, William Salomon, Brother Sam SSF, Sarah Simpson, Sarah and John Snyder, Janet Soskice, Gillian Spence, John Swinton, Gabby Thomas, Graham Tomlin, Giles Waller, Jim Walters, Daniel Weiss, Justin and Caroline Welby, Christina Weltz, Andy Wolfe, John Wood, Alexandra Wright, Tom Wright, Jon, Sophie, Izzy, Maddie and George Young, Peter Young, Simeon Zahl and Laurie Zoloth.

Some of the groups and institutional settings that helped with the commentary have also continued to be important. My own Cambridge worship community, St Andrew's Church, Cherry Hinton, has been especially significant. Not only did our vicar Karin Voth Harman initiate and lead, with the support of our curates Jeanine Bossy and Jon Sanders, a whole 'Year of John' in the parish (2022–2023) with a wide variety of events (including sessions with Jeremy Begbie, Rob McDonald and Maggi Dawn) but she also enabled, as she describes in her foreword, the 'road-testing' of the first five chapters of this book with a group of church members who gave substantial feedback. My thanks go also to all who took part in that group. The Lyn's House community of friends is still at the heart of my life, and my gratitude to its members is immense. The Monastery of St Barnabas the Encourager, the Community of St Anselm in Lambeth Palace, Chemin Neuf, the Theological Retreat Group accompanying Justin Welby, the Rose Castle Foundation, the Benedictine sisters of St Mary's Abbey in West Malling, the McDonald Agape Foundation,

Faith in Leadership, the Elijah Institute and the multi-faith Scriptural Reasoning community have all continued to contribute in valuable ways.

Part of the overflow of publishing the commentary has been the opportunity to engage with a wider range of groups and settings, which has been fruitful in many ways. My warm thanks to St Augustine's College, Canterbury; the Community at the Crossing, Cathedral of St John the Divine, New York; the Scottish Episcopal Diocese of St Andrews, Dunkeld and Dunblane; the members of Apostolic Reformation; a series of gatherings sponsored by the Bible Society in Westminster, Liverpool Cathedral and Swindon; Coventry Cathedral and the clergy of Coventry Diocese; the Canons of Ely Cathedral; the Licensed Lay Ministers of Ely Diocese; the retired clergy of Ely Diocese; Trinity Forum; the Scriptorium at the Church of St Edward King and Martyr; the Universities of Durham, Aberdeen and King's College London; the group in Harrogate with Graham Jones, and the Harrogate School of Theology with Stewart Davies; the clergy and licensed lay ministers of the Diocese of St Edmundsbury and Ipswich, led by Martin Seeley, their bishop; Ruomin Liu, whose translation of the commentary into Chinese, sponsored by the Bible Society, has now been completed; the men and women of the Benedictine community of Mucknell Abbey; the Anglican Parish of Furneaux Islands in Australia, where its two main churches, St Barnabas' in Lady Barron and St Alban's in Whitemark, studied and responded to an early draft of the first five chapters of this book, led by their locum priest Revd Dr Stephen Plant (Dean of Trinity Hall, Cambridge); and Laity Lodge in Texas, where Steve Purcell invited Micheal O'Siadhail and me to give a retreat. And a special word of thanks is due to the St Edmundsbury Cathedral clergy and the two cathedral Lent groups that road-tested the first five chapters and gave helpful feedback.

There have also been academic responses to the commentary on John. The reviews of the commentary in a number of journals have led me to reconsider many points. So too have two substantial panel responses – one at the British New Testament Society in St Andrews University in August 2022, where Andy Byers chaired a session to which Richard Bauckham, Catrin Williams and Andrew Lincoln contributed; the other at the November 2022 Annual Meeting of the Society for Biblical Literature in Denver, where Steve Fowl chaired a session with Katherine Sonderegger, Laura Sweat Holmes, Jim Fodor and Sosa Siliezar (their contributions and my response to them have now been published in the *Journal of Anglican Studies*). In Tübingen University, there was a discussion of the commentary led by Johanna Rahner, Professor of Catholic Theology. In the *Journal of Theological Interpretation*, Walter Moberly reviewed it, and I responded. It is so easy for a book to be ignored, and I greatly appreciate the quality of attention given to mine by so many, which has helped my work on this book.

At every point in the history of this book, Philip Law of SPCK has been the most considerate and patient publisher imaginable.

Likewise, Deborah has been the most encouraging wife imaginable.

Finally, there are the two people to whom I owe most with regard to the actual writing of the book. Micheal O'Siadhail has been the first reader of my writing for over fifty years (and I have been the first reader of his poetry), and he read and responded to every part of this book as it was written. This has been the first book of mine for which Amiel Osmaston has accompanied me as a reader. Not only did she comment on every chapter but she also drew on her many years leading education for the Diocese of Carlisle in order to write the questions that accompany each chapter. I am deeply grateful to her and to Micheal for their perceptiveness, honesty and encouragement.

Introduction
Meeting, trusting, maturing

If you want practical suggestions about the many different ways in which you or your church could use Meeting God in John, *see the last section of this introduction. In brief, it is a versatile 'Lent plus' book which can take you beyond Lent, through Holy Week and into Eastertide. Use it for a Lent group, on your own, for a mix of group and individual study or as a basis for a series of up to 12 sermons. It can be used effectively at other times of year too.*

The Gospel of John's two purposes

Now Jesus did many other signs in the presence of his disciples, which are not written in this book. But these are written so that you may come to believe that Jesus is the Messiah, the Son of God, and that through believing you may have life in his name. (John 20:30–31)

The Gospel of John is very clear about the twofold purpose for which it has been written.

The first purpose is 'so that you may come to believe and trust that Jesus is the Messiah, the Son of God.'[1] This involves being introduced to who Jesus is, meeting him through stories of what he did and said and what happened to him, and coming to trust him and know who he is. Just before this summary of the Gospel's purpose, John tells of Thomas meeting the resurrected Jesus and crying out to him, 'My Lord and my God!' (John 20:28). So to meet Jesus is to meet God.

1

The second purpose is 'that through believing and trusting you may have life in his name'. This involves long-term, ongoing trust and commitment. It is about maturing into a life-giving relationship with someone who says, 'I am the way, and the truth, and the life' (14:6). Right from the beginning and all through the Gospel, Jesus is identified with life, and that life is in turn identified with light, hunger and food, thirst and drink, truth, spirit, breath, peace, joy, love, glory and resurrection – the overcoming of death itself. As Jesus sums up his own purpose: 'I came that they may have life, and have it abundantly' (10:10).

John's Gospel is about meeting and trusting God through meeting and trusting Jesus, and then maturing into that core relationship of being loved and learning to love, open to the superabundance of life that he gives. This book, *Meeting God in John*, invites readers, through the Gospel of John, into that meeting, trusting and maturing. Inspired by John's Gospel, it is an introduction to who Jesus is and what 'life in his name' is like – life in deepening relationship with Jesus.

A Gospel for beginners and the more experienced

One very striking thing about John's Gospel is how well it is crafted both to be understood on first reading and to be inexhaustibly rich for those who reread and reread it.

On the one hand, it is written in simpler Greek than the other Gospels (and far simpler than Paul's Letters). It uses basic, easily understood ideas and images. Besides the life-related ones we already mentioned, we find word, darkness, blindness, desire, water, wine, bread, shepherd, scent, birth, death, washing, healing, trust, father, mother, child and more. It tells fewer but usually longer, carefully shaped and accessible stories. And it has a good deal of repetition, which allows key points to become clearer and to have more impact.

Yet, on the other hand, it is wonderfully deep and generative. Who can ever fully fathom the meaning of any of those words just listed? They are both immediately understandable and endlessly fascinating. As John uses them, they invite us to stretch our minds, imaginations and hearts and to open our lives to new dimensions of reality. Little, ordinary words can grip us and draw us into more and more meaning. 'This is my commandment, that you love one another as I have loved you' (15:12). What is the meaning of that 'as'? Or what is the meaning of 'in' in 'so that the love with which you have loved me may be in them, and I in them' (17:26)? The testimony of experienced readers for two millennia, all round the world, is that such a text is extraordinarily fruitful and continually challenging. There is always more to be found through it, more to grow into, more to surprise us.

There is a person, a name, at the heart of all this: Jesus. Jesus is utterly human like us. Jesus is also utterly one with God. God is free to express who God is in this way, and he has done so. God is free to give God's self to us in this person, and he has done so. That is the good news. We can never fully take it in or comprehend Jesus. The Gospel of John lets us meet Jesus, invites us to trust and love Jesus, and then challenges us to mature, expand and deepen our trust, understanding and love without limit.

The text of John's Gospel is crafted to achieve this by combining simplicity and depth. It is for both beginners and the more experienced. As the folk saying puts it, 'Mice can paddle and elephants can swim' in this Gospel. I hope that the following chapters might encourage both those at the beginning and those further along, and that all will be stimulated to go further and deeper through habitual rereading of John's Gospel. It is a habit that I and many others have found extraordinarily fruitful. The sheer overwhelming superabundance of this Gospel means that the difference between beginners and the more experienced seems tiny in comparison with the immensity of the meaning, love and glory we are all trying to fathom. It is something like the difference between the heights of a mouse and an elephant in comparison with the distance between both of them and the sun, the light of the world.

In order to help to enable both beginners and the more experienced, *Meeting God in John* is about both beginning and continuing, meeting and maturing, with no limit set to our growth in learning, loving and praying.

Chapter 1, 'The big picture: Meaning, love, Jesus', opens up the astonishing understanding of reality with which John's Gospel begins. Its Prologue, 1:1–18, has been perhaps the single most influential short passage during two millennia of Christianity, and it is as important as ever today.

The next three chapters of *Meeting God in John* begin from three core questions. These are first raised in the rest of the first chapter of John's Gospel, they are relevant throughout the Gospel and they can be seen as fundamental to Christian living. In this book, chapter 2 asks the question of identity, 'Who are you?'; chapter 3 asks the question of desire, 'What are you looking for?'; and chapter 4 asks the question of home, 'Where are you staying/dwelling/abiding?'

Chapter 5 is the culminating one for Lent as we approach Holy Week. It is centred on glory, as opened up in John 12, where Jesus prays, 'Father, glorify your name', and then a voice comes from heaven, 'I have glorified it, and I will glorify it again' (12:28). This goes to the heart of meeting God in John. John 17, the extraordinary outpouring of Jesus to his Father in prayer on the night before his death, then reveals the depths of their relationship. It opens up the intensity and intimacy of their mutual glorifying and loving. And, astonishingly, Jesus invites us all to share in that life.

The next three chapters, part 2 of *Meeting God in John*, are on 'The hour happens' – the climactic events of Holy Week and then Easter. Chapter 6 is on 'Thursday: Loving utterly, intimately, vulnerably, mutually', chapter 7 is on 'Friday: Jesus dies' and chapter 8 is on 'Sunday: Jesus alive'.

Part 3 is on 'The ongoing drama: Jesus happening in the twenty-first century'. Chapter 9, on 'Christian essentials now: Jesus and learning, praying, loving', distils from John's Gospel wisdom for Christian living today. All this culminates in the conclusion, 'Our future: Sent as Jesus was sent'. This summarises the astonishing vocation Jesus gives to his followers. It is a spirituality for our time.

How to use *Meeting God in John*

Overall, *Meeting God in John* can be read as a 'Lent plus' book. It is meant for individuals or groups who want a book that can be a companion through Lent and also, if desired, through Holy Week, into the Easter season and beyond. It has grown out of over twenty years spent on *The Gospel of John. A Theological Commentary* (which was published by Baker Academic in 2021). The commentary was written in order to be as accessible as possible in a style similar to this book (see the preface for more). Some readers might wish to follow through questions and themes by reading the commentary. From time to time, I will give references to assist in this.

But my main hope for this book is that, whether accompanied by the commentary or not, it might inspire readers, and even whole groups, congregations and communities, to become habitual rereaders of the Gospel of John itself.

It might be helpful for readers if I give some of my thoughts about how *Meeting God in John* might be used. These are suggestions only and are not meant to be prescriptive. I have imagined three sorts of reader or ways of reading this book.

One is an individual reader who follows the Church year, whether a beginner in relation to this Gospel or further along in understanding it. As has often been noted, John's Gospel itself is more concerned with the individual than the other Gospels. If someone is reading it as a 'Lent plus' book, the preface and introduction might be read at the beginning of Lent; the first five chapters during Lent before Holy

Week; chapters 6–7 during Holy Week; chapter 8 on Easter Sunday or during the following week; and then chapter 9 and the conclusion in the Easter season leading up to Ascension, Pentecost and Trinity Sunday. Then after that, as the Church enters a long period of 'ordinary time', readers who want to become habitual rereaders of John are offered one way of doing this in Alan Ecclestone's pattern of reading through John every ninety days (see appendix B).

Another way of reading this book is to be part of a Lent group, whether connected to a church or not. It is increasingly popular for local congregations of different denominations to organise Lent groups together, and the Gospel of John is an ideal ecumenical text (see especially John 17:20–26). I hear of a great variety of other kinds of Lent groups – women's groups, men's groups, friendship groups, work-based groups, interest-based groups, youth groups, peace-building groups, pub groups and more. Often, such groups have five meetings during Lent, and I have prepared chapters 1–5 with these in mind. Lent groups often have no meetings during Holy Week. So from chapter 6 onwards, I am imagining members continuing, if they wish, as individuals – perhaps reading chapters 6–7 in Holy Week, chapter 8 on Easter Sunday or during the following week and chapter 10 and the conclusion in the weeks leading up to Ascension, Pentecost and Trinity Sunday. This could be followed by reading short passages of John's Gospel daily, in line with the appendix.

The third way of reading this book is to read it at any time of year, completely unconnected with the pattern of the Church Year that is assumed in the first two. I hope that this book will be a suitable companion to anyone who is interested in God, or in Jesus, or in being a Christian, or in what it might mean to have a Christian worldview today, or simply in reflecting on one of the most influential texts in world history. For those who meet the Gospel of John mainly in short passages as part of church services, it is easy to forget that taken as a whole it is a very good read – and quite short. Indeed, I would urge every reader to read the whole Gospel slowly as the ideal preparation for the rest of the book.

Clergy and other church leaders might wish to use *Meeting God in John* as resource material to think and pray with as they prepare sermons and services during an intensively busy time of year.

1 If your church has no Lent group (or the group is using other material), you could use *Meeting God in John* as the basis for a series of five weekly sermons and services during Lent (chapters 1–5), perhaps followed by services or reflections on Maundy Thursday (chapter 6), Good Friday (chapter 7) and Easter day (chapter 8), with additional, flexible resources that can be used after Easter (chapter 9 and conclusion).

2 If your church does have one or more Lent groups and decides to use chapters 1–5 of *Meeting God in John*, then you might wish to follow this up with using material from chapters 6–9 for sermons and services from Palm Sunday onwards through Easter and towards Pentecost and Trinity.

3 If you already have other topics, material or plans for your church during Lent, Holy Week and Easter, then *Meeting God in John* might suit home group study or a series of sermons at a different time of year.

Part I

LENT

The Prologue of the Gospel of John, its first eighteen verses, gives a framework for understanding the whole of reality within which Christian living can happen – our learning, thinking and imagining, praying and worshipping, loving and serving. The first chapter in part 1 explores how the Prologue gives the essentials of a God-centred worldview for the twenty-first century.

The following three chapters respond in turn to the three essential questions raised by the Gospel of John. They are about who Jesus is and who we are; what we desire and orient our lives towards; and where we are most deeply and fully committed and at home. Then, chapter 5 culminates Lent by drawing together the first four chapters and opening up the main subject of this book: meeting God in John.

1

The big picture: Meaning, love, Jesus

The big picture of God and all reality, framing the whole Gospel of John, is given in its opening eighteen verses, the Prologue. This has probably been the single most important short text in the past two thousand years of Christian life and thought. I suggest that you read it very slowly.

In the beginning was the Word, and the Word was with God, and the Word was God. He was in the beginning with God. All things came into being through him, and without him not one thing came into being. What has come into being in him was life, and the life was the light of all people. The light shines in the darkness, and the darkness did not overcome it. There was a man sent from God, whose name was John. He came as a witness to testify to the light, so that all might believe through him. He himself was not the light, but he came to testify to the light. The true light, which enlightens everyone, was coming into the world. He was in the world, and the world came into being through him; yet the world did not know him. He came to what was his own, and his own people did not accept him. But to all who received him, who believed in his name, he gave power to become children of God, who were born, not of blood or of the will of the flesh or of the will of man, but of God. And the Word became flesh and lived among us, and we have seen his glory, the glory as of a father's only son, full of grace and truth.

(John testified to him and cried out, 'This was he of whom I said, "He who comes after me ranks ahead of me because he was before me."') From his fullness we have all received, grace upon grace. The law indeed was given through Moses; grace and truth came through Jesus Christ. No one has ever seen God. It is God the only Son, who is close to the Father's heart, who has made him known.

(John 1:1–18)

That can feel overwhelming, and so it should. It opens up a vast vision, like the texts scrolling down the screen at the beginning of a *Star Wars* film. The Prologue is about big realities, and the rest of the Gospel of John tells us more and more about them. We do not need to understand them all at once; we are starting a journey, and all we need is to be open to going further, a step at a time, a verse at a time. These things are so deep and broad that we never come to the end of them. They are meant to stretch our minds and hearts together and to shape the whole of our lives day by day. The message John gives here is clear: this glorious reality is what we are actually part of.

At the heart of this big picture are three fundamentals: meaning, love and Jesus.

Meaning

What a beginning!

The first five verses are about meaning. Words have meaning, and *the Word of God is about the deepest and fullest meaning.* This opening is about God and all reality, all things, all life, all people. They say that the world we live in is not meaningless; it makes deep sense. We can be confident that meaning and purpose really can be found. Even though there is also darkness and much that is not clear, there is light to see by.

How do we make sense of ourselves, of other people and of the world? Think of all the carriers of meaning in our lives. Language is crucial, and it is essential to the meaning, understanding and knowledge that we have. But there are many other carriers of meaning – smiles and frowns, gestures and actions, photographs and paintings, music and sport, food and drink, buildings and statues, clothes, hairstyles and nail art. There are also fields of meaning and knowledge such as history, archaeology, art, drama, literature, film, the sciences, technology and medicine. There are skills, practices and habits that are vital to ongoing life in society. (Which are most important to you?) Communities, organisations and institutions such as families, industries, businesses, the media, police and law courts, the armed forces, hospitals and surgeries, governments and civil services, schools and universities, sports and other clubs, charities of many sorts and international bodies – they are all carriers of meaning. (Which are you part of? Which affect you most?)

Then there are whole cultures, developed over centuries, through which millions find meaning. And there are the religions, philosophies, worldviews and ways of living that try to make sense of reality as a whole. There is no outsider way of proving which of these might be true. It is more a matter of slow learning, wise insight, decision-making about whom and what to trust, and finding what rings true by being involved. It is not just about knowledge with proof (important though that can be). We usually grow up in one religion, worldview or set of values (or sometimes a mixture), and learn it, try it out, question it, test it and sometimes change it, deepen it, reject it or find another that rings more true. (What has your experience been? Why are you reading this book?)

The Prologue of John's Gospel offers a framework for understanding reality that has been thought about, questioned, tested, trusted and lived for two thousand years by billions of people, and this is still continuing around the world. For me, as a scholar and a theologian, one of the most fascinating and educational things I have done is being editor of three editions and consultant to the fourth edition of a textbook[1] that introduces readers to the extraordinary story of Christian thinking from 1918 onwards. It has, in my judgement, been the most lively century in the whole history of Christian thought. In appendix C, I list the topics in the fourth edition so that you can have some sense of what has been going on. These topics show today's thinking on the scope of the first five verses of John's Gospel. There are voices of men and women from different Christian churches, numerous ethnicities, cultures and languages, many academic fields in the arts and sciences, and every continent. They range throughout the Bible, Christian ethics and spirituality and engagements with popular culture, secular thinking, other religions, economics, race, politics and the environmental crisis. Overwhelming indeed!

What have I learned from decades of trying to think and live the meaning opened up by these first five verses of the Gospel of John? Of many lessons, here are the three that are most relevant to the present book.

1 The Prologue of John's Gospel rings even more true in the light of modern understanding. It offers the framework for a worldview – centred on deep meaning, deep love and Jesus – that has been inhabited and tested for two thousand years. This continues to inspire deep and broad thinking and wisdom-seeking.

2 By far the most important thing is the desire to know God and to be open to the surprising message of this Gospel about meeting God through meeting Jesus. The first question of Jesus to his first followers ('disciples' simply means 'learners') is, 'What are you looking for?' (John 1:38). What do you desire? This Gospel offers an education in desire that leads to deep fulfilment.

3 The journey of learning goes on and on, and the Gospel of John is a reliable companion on it. It is a Gospel that is good for beginners and good for those who are further on. Reading and rereading it is a lifetime's occupation, with more and more meaning

and truth to be found. We never have a neat, final package of clear meaning. There is also absence of meaning: darkness. The Gospel is utterly realistic about darkness – suffering, death, sin, lies and evil. The light shines in darkness, but the darkness, as we all know, continues. But darkness does not have the last word. The last word is the Word of God, and 'in him was life, and the life was the light of all people. The light shines in the darkness, and the darkness did not overcome it' (1:4–5).

Love

What an ending!

'God the only Son, who is close to the Father's heart' (1:18). This is about *the deepest and fullest love*.

Through the rest of the Gospel, the love between Jesus and the One who sent him, first mentioned explicitly in John 3:35 ('The Father loves the Son and has placed all things in his hands'), emerges as the root of all reality, going back to before creation (17:5, 23–26). The vivid picture (translating the Greek literally) is of the Son 'in the bosom', 'on the breast' of the Father. It is an image that recurs at two crucial points, focused on 'the disciple whom Jesus loved' (13:23;[2] 21:20). That anonymous disciple, traditionally named John, to whom the writing of this Gospel is attributed (21:24), can be seen as a model for all discipleship, with an identity centred on trust, truth and love. Here, the 'Son, who is close to the Father's heart', is the source of that love.

Jesus

What a centre!

'And the Word became flesh and lived among us, and we have seen his glory, the glory as of a father's only son, full of grace and truth' (1:14). This is about *meeting God*. The Word has already been identified with God – 'the Word was God' (1:1). Now, the Word is embodied in human flesh and soon identified as 'Jesus Christ'. This is a momentous surprise, a singular, unprecedented event, a unique person. He is news. No wonder the Prologue (and the rest of the Gospel) repeatedly emphasises the importance of trusting testimony. '[John] came as a witness to testify to the light, so that all might believe and trust through him … John testified to him and cried out' (1:7–15). If we have not ourselves been present as eyewitnesses, we can only know news by trusting testimony.

In John's Gospel, the headline for meeting God is the testimony of eyewitnesses to Jesus: 'we have seen his glory' (1:15). But a key message of this Gospel is that to meet God through Jesus, it is not at all necessary to have been an eyewitness. This is made very clear at the end (see 20:24–31) when Thomas refuses to believe the testimony of his fellow disciples. He insists on seeing the resurrected Jesus. When he sees and believes, he cries out the climactic truth of the Gospel: 'My Lord and my God!' (20:28). But then Jesus says, 'Have you believed and trusted because you have seen me? Blessed are those who have not seen and yet have come to believe' (20:29). We who have not seen can be blessed by believing and trusting. John immediately goes on to address us readers:

> Now Jesus did many other signs in the presence of his disciples, which are not written in this book. But these are written so that you may come to believe and trust that Jesus is the Messiah, the Son of God, and that through believing and trusting you may have life in his name.
> (John 20:30–31)

This was the text that opened my introduction, and you might wish to reread that on meeting, trusting and maturing. That is immensely important for those of us who want to meet God in John today. Thomas's cry to the crucified and resurrected Jesus, 'My Lord and my

God!' identifies Jesus as the One who is present now as he was then. Our reading now is done in the presence of Jesus. To Thomas, he was visible; to us, he is invisible. We can be among those who receive the blessing of Jesus on 'those who have not seen and yet have come to believe.' John's purpose in writing is for us readers to come to trust Jesus and for that relationship to be permanent – to 'have life in his name'.

Jesus is central not only to the Prologue but to the whole of this Gospel, the other Gospels and the rest of the New Testament. Who Jesus is is the key question in every chapter of John's Gospel, and the next chapter of this book will explore the question further. But first, we look at the key message about him in the Prologue and the rest of the Gospel, which is the message central to this book: that meeting Jesus is meeting God.

Meeting Jesus, meeting God

For John, and for the Christian community that follows him, the reality in which we live is one of abundant meaning and abundant love, and at the heart of this is a living person who embodies the deepest meaning and the deepest love. *Jesus is the free self-expression of God, the Word of God.*

Later, in the first explicit mention of love in this Gospel, Jesus says, 'For God so loved the world that he gave his only Son, so that everyone who believes and trusts in him may not perish but may have eternal life' (3:16). *Jesus is also the free, self-giving of God in love.*

In Jesus, God 'became flesh and lived among us' (1:14), and, say the first eyewitnesses, 'we have seen his glory' (1:15). But that visible presence – in one time and place, to a limited number of eyewitnesses such as Mary Magdalene and Thomas in John 20 – came to an end. Then his invisible, permanent presence became available to unlimited numbers of people in all places and times.

This is vividly seen in what is perhaps the most moving meeting with Jesus in John's Gospel, when Mary Magdalene, who has seen Jesus die, is weeping at his empty tomb, looking for his dead body. Instead of finding his body, she is found by the living Jesus, risen from death. 'Jesus said to her, "Mary!" She turned and said to him in Hebrew, "Rabbouni!" (which means Teacher). Jesus said to her, "Do not hold on to me, because I have not yet ascended to the Father"' (20:16–17).

Holding on to him was possible for her then and there. But he was ascending to be, as the Prologue says, 'close to the Father's heart' (1:18). There, he is divinely free to relate permanently to her and to everyone else. This is the relationship that, in the parable of the vine, his disciples are invited into by Jesus: 'Abide in me as I abide in you' (15:4). In his final prayer, he prays for this permanent relationship of trust and love for 'those who will believe in me ... As you, Father, are in me and I am in you, may they also be in us, so that the world may believe and trust that you have sent me' (17:20–21). So Mary – and anyone else who trusts Jesus – could have a far better relationship than seeing and holding on physically to Jesus, one that could be compared with the deepest relationship of all: the love between Jesus and his Father.

That meeting with Mary is just one of many meetings with Jesus that are described in the Gospels. John's Gospel has fewer such encounters than the others, but those it does give are often told at greater length and in greater depth and are selected to teach the essentials. We will try to enter as deeply as possible into some of these meetings in later chapters, and each of them can be a way of meeting with God through Jesus.[3]

The last verse of the Prologue says that 'no one has ever seen God', but that Jesus Christ 'has made him known'. That knowledge comes through meeting Jesus in person. Sometimes, it is the actions of Jesus that are most revealing; sometimes it is his words; sometimes it is the responses of other people to him. But always, in every chapter of

John's Gospel as in the Prologue, the central issue is clear: *who Jesus is*. We will turn to that in our next chapter

Conclusion

The Christian worldview that is opened up in the Prologue of John's Gospel is one of deep meaning and deep love embodied in Jesus. It is always Jesus in relationship – with God as his Father, with all humanity, with each person and with the whole creation. Within that horizon, it gives readers the most important and far-reaching invitation imaginable: to meet, trust and go on trusting Jesus, maturing in learning, praying and loving. We now turn to the question of identity – his and ours.

Questions for individual reflection and group discussion

Suggested by Revd Canon Amiel Osmaston.

1 'The Word became flesh and lived among us, and we have seen his glory, the glory as of a father's only son, full of grace and truth … No one has ever seen God. It is God the only Son, who is close to the Father's heart, who has made him known' (John 1:14–18). As you think of Jesus (in the Bible and in your experience), what has Jesus shown you about God?

2 In the Gospels, is there any particular person, situation or story which speaks to you most strongly about responding to Jesus, trusting him and following him? Why is it meaningful for you?

3 David Ford writes in his introduction to this book, 'John's Gospel is about meeting and trusting God through meeting and trusting Jesus, and then maturing into that core relationship of being loved and learning to love, open to the superabundance of

life that he gives.' Can you remember any occasion or experience when Jesus has seemed particularly 'real and alive' to you?

4 The Christian worldview and understanding of true reality, of what life is ultimately all about, is radically different from many aspects of our multi-faith and multi-secular Western culture. Can you think of some of the main ways in which they conflict? How should we respond as Christians?

2

Identity: 'Who are you?'

We have begun to enter into the horizon of God and all reality opened up by the Prologue of John's Gospel. It is about deep meaning and deep love, both found in Jesus.

Immediately after the Prologue comes the first question in the Gospel: 'Who are you?' (1:19). Questions are very important all through this Gospel and through the rest of the Bible. They are especially important in the rest of John 1 because this is when Jesus begins to gather his disciples. Disciple (Greek *mathētēs*, Latin *discipulus*) simply means 'learner'. So, Jesus is gathering a community of learners.

In any learning community, good, stimulating questions are vital. The art of asking and pursuing perceptive, deep questions is one of the great skills in life. It is worth asking ourselves regularly, 'What are the leading questions that actually inspire us?'

The three leading questions in John 1 run all through the rest of the Gospel and all through life:

1 Who are you? The question of identity is the subject of this chapter, with the main focus on Jesus and the Samaritan woman who meets him.
2 What are you looking for? The question of desire in John 1:38 is the subject of chapter 3.
3 Where are you staying/abiding? The question of long-term dwelling, living and relationship – where we are most at home – is the subject of chapter 4.

All three come together in chapter 5, 'Glory: Meeting God in John'.

Who are you?

After the Prologue, the drama of the Gospel opens with sharp questions and answers. The question, 'Who are you?' is not asked just once but again and again. It is addressed to John the Baptist by representatives of the central Jewish authorities in Jerusalem sent to interrogate him. His repeated 'I am not' (1:20, 21) directs attention away from himself and towards Jesus. John the Baptist sees himself as 'the voice of one crying out in the wilderness, "Make straight the way of the Lord"' (1:23).

That is an extraordinary statement to make about someone: John is saying that the one for whom he is preparing the way is none other than 'the Lord' – God! As the interrogation continues, he goes further in identifying an actual person: 'Among you stands one whom you do not know, the one who is coming after me; I am not worthy to untie the thong of his sandal' (1:26–27).

That completes the shift of focus from John to the 'who' coming after him. Within the story, for the priests and Levites questioning John, this is 'one whom you do not know'. For readers of the Prologue, where John has been introduced as the leading witness to Jesus, it is clear who this 'who' is: the Word of God in person, Jesus Christ, 'close to the Father's heart'.

The next event is the appearance of Jesus himself for the first time, with John announcing who Jesus is: 'Here is the Lamb of God who takes away the sin of the world … a man who ranks ahead of me because he was before me … He on whom you see the Spirit descend and remain is the one who baptizes with the Holy Spirit … this is the Son of God' (1:29–34).

Then comes a stream of ways of identifying who Jesus is: 'Rabbi' (meaning 'teacher'); 'Messiah' (meaning 'anointed'); 'him about whom Moses in the law and also the prophets wrote, Jesus son of

Joseph from Nazareth'; 'Rabbi' again; 'Son of God' again; 'King of Israel'; and – the only one on the lips of Jesus himself – 'Son of Man' (1:38–51).

What has happened? *The leading question of this Gospel, 'Who are you?', has been raised about John the Baptist, who then dramatically redirects it towards Jesus, and the main focus stays on Jesus for the rest of the Gospel.* 'Who is Jesus?' is the core question, explicit or implicit, in every single chapter. It is a question that follows obviously from the Prologue, which has introduced Jesus as central to finding the meaning of the reality we live in.

The repeated 'I am not' of John the Baptist prepares for the repeated 'I am' of Jesus later in the Gospel. Those are the most obvious pointers to the identity of Jesus, but there are many others. Sometimes, who Jesus is is communicated through his actions, sometimes through his words, sometimes through the responses of others to him, and always by the way the author tells the story and comments on it. For this book, his meetings have a special relevance. So the main text studied in this chapter is an encounter with a woman in which both the identity of Jesus and her identity are significant. This has consequences for the deep and controversial questions of identity that are so important today and, above all, for the 'who-to-who' meeting of God with each of us.

Jesus meets a Samaritan woman (John 4:1–42)

First, read the story of Jesus meeting a Samaritan woman in John 4:1–42. If you are in a group, I suggest that you let each member share one key word or phrase and notice how differently the account strikes people. The leading question in what follows is about identity: who Jesus is, who the woman is and what this meeting might mean for us and our identity now.

Who is Jesus?

By the time we reach John 4, readers have already been introduced to Jesus as the most important imaginable person – at one with God, at one with humanity, involved with all creation, described in a series of striking titles, sent to the world in love, doing 'signs' of abundant life and gathering a community of disciples who trust him. His meeting with the Samaritan woman and her community reveals more about who he is and what he means.

The issue of identity is clear from the start of their conversation. 'How is it that you, a Jew, ask a drink of me, a woman of Samaria? (Jews do not share things in common with Samaritans)' (4:9). He is being controversial in two ways: as a Jew engaging across a religious and ethnic identity division and as a man opening a conversation with a strange woman against the norms of that culture. The response of his disciples to finding him talking with her is to be 'astonished that he was speaking with a woman' (4:27). So Jesus is someone who is not afraid to relate across the usual boundaries of religion, ethnicity, gender and culture. It is worth asking ourselves how we relate across those boundaries.

The reply of Jesus emphasises his own identity even more but not as Jewish and male. 'Jesus answered her, "If you knew the gift of God, and who it is that is saying to you, "Give me a drink", you would have asked him, and he would have given you living water"' (4:10). This centres his identity in God and an image of abundant life.

For the woman, his mysterious statement about living water begins a conversation that then moves in leaps towards an eventual climactic new identification of Jesus by her whole Samaritan community: 'Saviour of the world'.

First, Jesus promises 'a spring of water gushing up to eternal life' (4:14). Next, he opens up her marriage history (4:16–18). Then, she comes to a new perception of who Jesus is: 'Sir, I see that you are a prophet' (4:19).

She also raises a painfully divisive question between Jews and Samaritans: where should worship be centred? But Jesus refuses to recognise this religious division as important, and defines worship by who God is, not where the worshipper is: 'The hour is coming, and is now here, when the true worshippers will worship the Father in spirit and truth … God is spirit, and those who worship him must worship in spirit and truth' (4:23–24). For those who reread this knowing the rest of the Gospel, this too is about the God-centred identity of Jesus, who can say, 'I am … the truth' (14:6) and is the giver of the Holy Spirit (20:22).

The woman then speaks of her expectation of the Messiah, Christ, and this draws the most surprising and significant of all responses from Jesus: 'I am he [Greek *egō eimi*], the one who is speaking to you' (4:26). *That Greek phrase, meaning simply 'I am', is the clearest way in which John, again and again, emphasises the central importance of who Jesus is.* It is how God is self-described in the foundational self-revelation to Moses at the burning bush, 'I AM WHO I AM' (Exodus 3:14), and in the Book of Isaiah. It identifies Jesus with God. God is present as Jesus, as the Prologue has said. Here, in John 4:26, this first 'I am' on the lips of Jesus can also mean, as the NRSV says, 'I am he', meaning, 'I am the Messiah (or the Christ)'. It is as if John is slipping it in for the first time without emphasising it, knowing that it could simply be taken as referring to Jesus as the Messiah. But, as the Gospel continues, it is used to describe Jesus repeatedly. Sometimes, the 'I am' is expanded by a description, as in 'I am the bread of life' (John 6:48); 'I am the light of the world' (8:12); 'I am the good shepherd' (10:11); 'I am the resurrection and the life' (11:25); 'I am the way, and the truth, and the life' (14:6); but sometimes (as literally in 4:26), it is used absolutely, perhaps most emphatically and dramatically in 8:58: 'Jesus said to them, "Very truly, I tell you, before Abraham was, I am."' That is the divine 'I am'.

But there is yet more about who Jesus is. When the disciples return, the woman leaves her water jar. This might possibly be a sign of commitment, like some of the first fishermen disciples in other Gospels who leave their nets. The woman goes and tells her story to her fellow Samaritans, invites them to come to see Jesus and tantalises them with her final question, 'He cannot be the Messiah, can he?' (4:29). Some believed/trusted/had faith in him because of her testimony and then were later confirmed in this by meeting him for themselves, and 'many more believed [trusted and had faith] because of his word' (4:41). Their culminating statement adds yet another title to the many others: 'we know that this is truly the Saviour of the world' (4:42). This is especially relevant to the Samaritans and to others beyond the Jewish people. 'Saviour' is both a Jewish term for God (for example, in Isaiah 43:3, 11; 45:12, 21) and what the Roman emperor was called, so it speaks to both Jews and non-Jews.

John is indicating *a God-centred and life-centred identity* more embracing than that of either Jew or non-Jew and uniting people across deep differences. This is first headlined in the Prologue: 'What has come into being in him was life, and the life was the light of all people ... to all who received him, who believed [trusted and had faith] in his name, he gave power to become children of God, who were born, not of blood or of the will of the flesh or of the will of man, but of God' (1:3–12). To be 'born ... of God' is to receive our life from God. This is to be the heart of who we are, more important than family, gender, race, culture or any other marker of identity. We receive power to be this by trusting in who Jesus is ('in his name'). What happens then is that we have a new family identity as 'children of God'. We are brothers, sisters and friends of Jesus, the Son of God. And at the heart of this is not only being born into this family but also maturing in it together. Its deepest, open secret is love: we are utterly loved and, as we trust that, we are inspired and taught by Jesus, 'the Son who is close to the Father's heart' (1:18), to live a life of daring love as he did.

A woman transformed

What about the Samaritan woman?

She has come to the well for water, and she finds there a tired Jesus who asks her for a drink. They share an identity as human beings who need water to live, and they are intimately connected with all other life that also depends on water.

In her superb *Earth Bible Commentary*, Margaret Daly-Denton sets this meeting in the ecological, economic, social and cultural context of its time. For example, she discusses water-carrying as a tedious daily task for women (as it still is for millions today) and environmental degradation in the Roman Empire. But she also again and again illuminates how water is a 'silver thread' through the Gospel of John,[1] one that resonates with the whole of Israel's Scriptures, and she makes profound and prophetic connections with life today and our environmental crisis. It is hard to overestimate how important it is for our century that Jesus is the one through whom 'all things came into being' (1:3), and that he came 'that they may have life, and have it abundantly' (10:10). Here in John 4, there is no playing down the need for literal, material water for life, but abundant life is more than this, and Jesus is offering the woman 'a spring of water gushing up to eternal life.'

Eternal life in John's Gospel is the deep, lasting life that is above all identified with who Jesus is and the gift of his Spirit. Jesus is present as God is present, he is the 'I am' who is on both sides of death, so this deep life can be entered now. As will be seen in later chapters of this book, it can be identified with light, love, joy, glory, truth, resurrection and more, but its character above all emerges through Jesus acting, teaching, engaging with people and, climactically, suffering, dying and rising from death. To be given this life is the ultimate gift, as the woman now begins to experience.

She is a receptive learner, who makes mistakes but is also open to discussing profound personal and religious matters.

First, her imagination is stirred and stretched by what Jesus says. He engages with her across the boundaries of her identity as a Samaritan woman; and he gives her a promise of vibrant, overflowing life pictured as water – something vital to everyone, whatever their particular identity. This opens the way into a deeper engagement with her as a woman and as a Samaritan.

Jesus then breaks an impasse in their conversation by going deep into her past as a wife and her current close relationship with a man: 'you have had five husbands, and the one you have now is not your husband' (4:18). Her eventual testimony to what has happened with Jesus is, 'Come and see a man who told me everything I have ever done!' (4:29). It implies that a lot has been left untold by John about this conversation and suggests something crucial about what can happen in meeting Jesus and God through Jesus: we are known through and through, and our whole lives and selves, in all their messiness, pain, joy and complication, are understood with compassion. This woman knows that she is known in a good way, for her own good. The climactic example of this compassion comes in the final chapter of John when Peter, who has denied Jesus, is gently given a completely fresh start in love and service, and can exclaim, 'Lord, you know everything' (21:17).

She next raises a key question for herself as a Samaritan and for Jesus as a Jew: worship of God. Again, Jesus goes deeper. She has already identified him as a prophet. Now, he first invites her further trust – 'Woman, believe [and trust] me' (4:21). Then, in a rich passage (4:21–26), he says that something new is happening: 'the hour is coming … the hour is coming, and is now.' That is worship beyond what either Samaritans or Jews have known up to now. And the culmination of this exchange makes clear that this momentous present event is inseparable from who Jesus is: 'I am.'

In this meeting, both her life as a woman and her worship as a Samaritan have been confronted by Jesus. Step by step, she learns who he is and finds her own identity transformed. In the final scene (4:39–42), her new life overflows in testimony to her fellow-Samaritans, they meet Jesus for themselves and a new community of trust in him is formed.

Conclusion

John 4:1–42 has told a story that raises profound questions of identity today. Some of these are given in the questions at the end of this chapter, and readers are invited to raise more.

But such questions of identity – of Jesus and God, of ourselves and our communities – will go on being relevant all through this Gospel, and they are especially interwoven with the leading questions of the following two chapters. Indeed, the story of Jesus and the Samaritan woman can act as an introduction to those two questions, and I conclude now by opening these up.

Relating to chapter 3, 'Desire: What are you looking for?', thirst is the most obvious form of desire for both Jesus and the Samaritan woman, with Jesus opening up for her other dimensions of thirst beyond that for literal water. There is also the desire for God that might be assumed to be implicit in worship. But, strikingly, the desire in relation to worship that is actually affirmed is that of God as Father seeking us: 'But the hour is coming, and is now here, when the true worshippers will worship the Father in spirit and truth, for the Father seeks such as these to worship him' (4:23). But the most emphatic statement on desire in this story comes in the conversation between Jesus and his disciples when they return bringing him food (4:27–38). They urge him to eat, but he says, 'My food is to do the will [Greek *thelēma*, meaning 'will, desire, wish, want'] of him who sent me and to complete his work' (4:34). That is a desire that goes to the heart of his most important relationship, with his Father, and the Gospel repeatedly invites readers to let this be their core desire too, above all in the prayer of Jesus in John 17.

Relating to our chapter 4 on 'Home: Where are you staying?', the final scene of Jesus with the Samaritans is revealing. 'So when the Samaritans came to him, they asked him to stay [Greek *meinai*] with them; and he stayed [Greek *emeinen*] there for two days' (4:40). Their deepening in faith happens through Jesus staying, abiding, dwelling with them.

Questions for individual reflection and group discussion

Suggested by Revd Canon Amiel Osmaston.

1 Looking at the story of Jesus' meeting with the Samaritan woman at the well, what seems to you the most significant way in which it reveals who Jesus is – his identity and character? Also, as we see Jesus speak to and relate to the woman, what does it show us about ourselves as we engage with Jesus?

2 The Samaritan woman was 'transformed' by her meeting with Jesus. Can you think of a person you know who has been transformed by meeting and following Jesus? What difference has it made in them?

3 'To all who received him, who believed [or trusted, or had faith] in his name, he gave power to become children of God' (John 1:12). David Ford writes, 'To be "born … of God" is to receive our life from God. This is to be the heart of who we are, more important than family, gender, race, culture or any other marker of identity.' Do you agree? Is this really possible for us?

4 John's Gospel records Jesus saying, 'I am the bread of life' (6:48), 'I am the light of the world' (8:12), 'I am the good shepherd' (10:11), 'I am the resurrection and the life' (11:25), 'I am the way, and the truth, and the life' (14:6). Which of these 'I am' statements or images speaks to you most vividly about the identity of Jesus? Why?

3

Desire: 'What are you looking for?'

'What are you looking for?' (Greek *ti zēteite*). These are, in the Gospel of John, the very first words of Jesus, the Word of God, to his first disciples. It is one of the most important questions anyone can ask: '*What do you desire?*' The Greek verb is very strong and multifaceted – look for, search for, seek out, strive for, want, ask for, demand, require, examine, expect, wish, desire. It is used all through John's Gospel along with other similar words, above all the key Greek verb *thelein*, meaning 'desire', 'wish', 'want' and 'will'.

The result is that this Gospel can be read as a drama of desire and an education in a wisdom of desire. Watch for this as you read and reread, and seek connections with life now.

A huge amount of our personal lives and our culture is about desire. Life is full of choices, decisions, hopes, fears, things we want and things we don't want, the need to prioritise this activity over that or to prefer relating to this person over relating to that person, possibilities for joining this or that group or movement, orienting our lives in one direction rather than another, or committing to a club or a cause or a person or a job or an ideal. *There has never been a culture more saturated by so many stimuli to desire through so many media*: click on this, vote for this, buy this, eat this, drink this, like this, watch this, read this, learn this, believe this, protest against this, visit this, imitate this, be like this, follow this person and so on. The people and organisations that are most successful in stimulating our desires are among the wealthiest and most powerful in the world. And, of course, our desires can go gloriously right, disastrously wrong or anything in between.

Desire in the Gospel of John

Jesus himself in his first words raises the question of desire with his new disciples, and that remains the most essential question addressed to both disciples and to us readers – though, as we will see, there is a crucial shift later from 'what' to 'who'.

At the well in Samaria, as we have seen, Jesus says that God his Father seeks people who will worship in spirit and truth (John 4:23–24) and that his own food is 'to do the will [or desire] of him who sent me' (4:34; see also 5:30). The purpose of the whole Gospel and each of its chapters is to draw us deeper and deeper into this drama of desire, inspiring us to devote ourselves more and more to desires that are in tune with the desires of Jesus.

This is a life-and-death drama. His enemies 'were seeking all the more to kill him' (5:18; see also 7:1, 19, 20, 25, 39; 8:37, 40; 10:39; 11:8). Then, when the final act of his life begins in the garden where he is arrested (18:1–8), Jesus asks a significant, repeated variation on his first words to his first disciples. He now puts 'who' in place of 'what'. Jesus asks them, 'For whom are you looking?', 'For whom are you looking?' (18:4, 7). They say, 'Jesus of Nazareth', 'Jesus of Nazareth' (18:5, 7). His answer is his signature identity, *'egō eimi', 'egō eimi', 'egō eimi'* (18:5, 6, 8), which can mean 'I am he' or simply 'I am'.

The point is powerfully reinforced in the first encounter with the resurrected Jesus, when his first words to Mary Magdalene are 'Woman, why are you weeping? For whom are you looking?' (20:15). *The question of identity and the question of desire have fused into the most important question of all, the 'who' question, focused on Jesus.*

The final two exchanges in the final chapter of John further deepen this Jesus-oriented and God-centred wisdom of desire.

First, Peter is repeatedly asked by Jesus, 'Do you love me?' and repeatedly affirms his love (21:15–17); he is repeatedly given his vocation as a pastor – 'Feed my sheep' (21:15, 17); and then is told this:

'Very truly, I tell you, when you were younger, you used to fasten your belt and to go wherever you wished [willed and desired (*thelein*)]. But when you grow old, you will stretch out your hands, and someone else will fasten a belt around you and take you where you do not wish [will and desire (*thelein* again)] to go.' (He said this to indicate the kind of death by which he would glorify God.) After this he said to him, 'Follow me.' (John 21:18–19)

Peter's desire to follow Jesus in a vocation of love and service to the glory of God is affirmed, but it means the sacrifice of some lesser desires. This is a key thought for Lent.

Then, Peter asks, 'What about him?' turning to 'the disciple whom Jesus loved' (21:20–23), whose closeness to Jesus at the Last Supper is recalled. Jesus says, 'If it is my will [wish and desire (*thelein*)] that he remain until I come, what is that to you? Follow me!' (21:22). Peter is given no overview of another disciple's future or of the timing or other details of the coming of Jesus. As usual with John's Gospel, there is a laser-like focus on the essentials, which in this case are:

1 The primacy of the desire/will of Jesus: 'my will/wish/desire'.
2 The key to the future is a person, Jesus: 'until I come'.
3 The way into that future is with this person, Jesus: 'Follow me!'

Peter's 'what' question has been given a triple who-centred answer, and his desire has been refocused on that centre – the 'my', 'I' and 'me' of Jesus.

So, overall, this is a drama in which many – often conflicting – desires interact.[1] The desires of Jesus, his Father, his disciples, his enemies, the crowd, worshippers and others are all in play, and readers are being repeatedly invited to let their desires be inspired, formed and transformed. We will now explore one key text that illuminates this theme.

The feeding of a large crowd: An education of desire (John 6:1–71)

Read John 6 slowly, noticing the ways in which it is teaching a wisdom of desire through the scenes of a mini drama.

Key 'desire' words include wanted (6:11, 21); looking for (6:24, 26); work for (6:27); hungry (6:35); thirsty (6:35); will/desire (6:38 ×2, 39, 40); and wish/desire (6:67).

Just as revealing are the number of 'food' and 'life' words, which point to what is desired: 'bread' (6:5, 7, 31, 32 ×2, 33, 34, 35, 41, 48, 50, 51, 58 ×2); loaves (6:9, 11, 26); fish (6:9, 11); fragments (6:12, 13); eaten, ate, eat (6:13, 23, 26, 49, 50, 51 ×2, 52, 53, 54, 56, 57, 58 ×2); food (6:27 ×2, 55); manna (6:31, 49); life, living, life (6:33, 40, 47, 48, 51 ×3, 53, 54, 57 ×3, 58, 63 ×2, 68); raise up (6:39, 40, 44, 54); and drink (6:53, 54, 55, 56).

Desire for health and food

'A large crowd kept following him, because they saw the signs that he was doing for the sick' (6:2). The desire for health is good and natural, and Jesus heals people as part of the abundant life he came to bring (a key statement on this is 10:10). But life is more than being free from illness. The healings, the feeding that is soon to happen and the other striking things Jesus does in his public ministry are not called 'miracles' in John's Gospel but 'signs'.

The signs of abundant life that Jesus does begin with him turning a huge amount of water into wine for everyone at a wedding (2:1–12), and the culmination is when he raises his friend Lazarus from death (11:1–44). Signs are good things in themselves, but they also point beyond themselves to what the headline in the Prologue says: 'From his fullness we have all received, grace upon grace' (1:16). There are many dimensions of that fullness, such as trust/belief/faith, truth, joy, prayer, service, love and glory.[2] There is rich imagery for it too, such as superabundant wine, water, wind/spirit, bread, fish, fruit, light and books. And the deepest meaning in all this is not so much what is received as who is received: the fullness is *his* and the 'we' who receive it are those 'who received *him*, who believed [or trusted] in *his* name' (1:12).

Jesus responds to the hunger of the crowd without them even mentioning it, and he meets it with an abundance of bread and fish. They are given 'as much as they wanted [and desired (*thelein*)]', and there is great emphasis on the amount left over: 'they filled twelve baskets'. So far so good.

Desire for power, food and signs versus desire for Jesus and the life he gives

But then comes conflict between what the crowd desires and what Jesus desires. The key issues are about power, food and signs that can convince people to believe.

On power, the crowd 'were about to come and take him by force to make him king.' They want a powerful leader to free them from Roman rule, which Jesus resists by withdrawing 'to the mountain by himself ' (6:15). The deeper meaning of this resistance comes out later during the trial of Jesus in his exchanges with Pontius Pilate (18:33–38). In reply to Pilate asking him whether he is King of the Jews, Jesus says, 'My kingdom is not from this world. If my kingdom were from this world, my followers would be fighting' (18:36). As he had just said to Peter, who had used his sword to resist Jesus being arrested, 'Put your sword back into its sheath. Am I not to drink the cup that the Father has given me?' (18:11). And, just before that, as he prepared his disciples for his death, he had taught them the meaning of that cup: 'No one has greater love than this, to lay down one's life for one's friends ... And for their sakes I sanctify myself, so that they also may be sanctified in truth' (15:13; 17:19). *He shows, and is, the truth of love.* Now, when Pilate asks again whether he is a king, he says, 'For this I was born, and for this I came into the world, to testify to the truth. Everyone who belongs to the truth listens to my voice' (18:37). *It is the attractive, non-coercive power of truth utterly at one with love.*

On food, the crowd that 'went to Capernaum looking for Jesus' are told:

Very truly, I tell you, you are looking for me, not because you saw signs, but because you ate your fill of loaves. Do not work for the food that perishes, but for the food that endures [lasts and abides (Greek *menein*)] for eternal life, which the Son of Man will give you.
(John 6:26–27)

Some desires need to be given priority, and Lent is a time of year to focus on these – here, desire for the deep, lasting, abundant life that Jesus gives. Jesus immediately begins to open up the deeper meaning of this: 'This is the work of God, that you believe [or trust or have faith] in him whom he [God the Father] has sent' (6:29). *Trust in Jesus is the basic key to right desire, to receiving the life he gives and to following wherever he leads.*

On signs, the people challenge Jesus: 'What sign are you going to give us, then, so that we may see it and believe [and trust] you?' (6:30). It is as if the quiet, one-off 'sign' of the feeding is not enough; they want something as spectacular as Moses giving the whole people manna in the wilderness day after day. Then the rest of the chapter leads, through a Jesus-centred understanding of that manna, towards the climactic sign in John's Gospel: the crucifixion of Jesus. 'The bread that I will give for the life of the world is my flesh' (6:51). That event is the strange, shocking, life-giving heart of desire, love, truth and glory in the Gospel of John. Or rather, *it is the person at the centre of that event who is at the heart of life, love, truth and glory, and who is to be desired and trusted utterly.* We will explore further as we approach Holy Week and the mystery of his attractive promise: 'And I, when I am lifted up from the earth, will draw all people to myself' (12:32).

Desire fulfilled – continually!

The whole chapter pivots around its central verse:

> Jesus said to them, 'I am the bread of life. Whoever comes to me will never be hungry, and whoever believes in me will never be thirsty.
> (John 6:35)

Jesus has just said that his Father is giving to those to whom he is speaking (in the synagogue in Capernaum, see 6:50) the gift of bread that is better than the manna they have said they want. In 6:32–33, he promises 'the true bread from heaven … the bread of God … which comes down from heaven and gives life to the world.' That exceeds what Moses gave in two ways. First, it is about more than satisfying physical hunger day by day; it is the gift of 'life', which he has just described as 'eternal life' (6:27) – deep, lasting, God-centred life. Second, it is not just for the people of Israel; this is life for 'the world'. It is life unlimited in quality, time and space. This stimulates their desire: 'Sir, give us this bread always' (6:34).

Then comes the decisive, astonishing affirmation beyond anything they could have imagined: 'Jesus said to them, "I am the bread of life. Whoever comes to me will never be hungry, and whoever believes [and trusts] in me will never be thirsty.' *The gift is a relationship of closeness and trust with this living person, whose 'I am' means his unity with God.*

What does this mean for desire? Does desire cease when it is fulfilled in this way? Of course not! Think of how vital the theme of marriage is in John's opening chapters – the first 'sign' of water turned into abundant wine at the wedding in Cana, Jesus as bridegroom, John the Baptist as friend of the bridegroom, and more.[3] In a good marriage, desire is both fulfilled and continues to be fulfilled, now in the context of a relationship of wholehearted and mutual trust and commitment. *In this pivotal verse 35, we – 'whoever' – are being invited to meet God through coming to Jesus, trusting him, living in this relationship permanently and desiring in line with his desires.* Above, we have already begun to open up the rich account in John 21 of matured desire in mutual trust, understanding and love, as seen in Peter and the Beloved Disciple.

The verses immediately after verse 35 make it very clear how fundamental desire is. Jesus sums up his whole purpose as being to do 'the will [and desire (*thelēma*)] of him who sent me', and that is then summed up as 'This is indeed the will [and desire (*thelēma*)] of my Father, that all who see the Son and believe [trust and have faith] in him may have eternal life; and I will raise them up on the last day' (6:40). That summary in terms of 'eternal life', for which I think the best description is 'deep, lasting, God-centred life', is, however, not the only one. As we will see in later chapters (of both John's Gospel and this book) and as has already been anticipated above, an even more important one is love. The shift to emphasising love begins in John 11 with the love between Jesus, Martha, Mary and Lazarus; it intensifies in the Farewell Discourses in John 13 – 17; and it culminates in John 21.

'Do you also wish to go away?' (John 6:67)

The rest of John 6 goes deeper into the meaning of verse 35. They are depths that have been the subject of bitter and sometimes violent disputes in Christian history, especially concerning how to understand the Eucharist (also known as the Lord's Supper, the Mass and Holy Communion). In this chapter, John too acknowledges how controversial and difficult these matters are, given such statements as 'Very truly, I tell you, unless you eat the flesh of the Son of Man and drink his blood, you have no life in you' (6:53). We will explore some of the issues in later chapters, but for now, there are two key things in the later part of John 6 to be noted.

One is the introduction of mutual abiding in Jesus: 'Those who eat my flesh and drink my blood abide in me, and I in them' (6:56). Such deep mutuality is the goal of meeting God in John. One way into realising this is to follow the practical suggestion at the beginning of this book and to pray the Lord's Prayer in the light of John 17.

The other is the final mention of desire. The way Jesus speaks of his flesh being eaten and his blood being drunk scandalises even many of his own disciples, so that they leave him. Then 'Jesus asked the twelve, "Do you also wish [and desire (*thelein*)] to go away?"' (6:67). This rings true with the whole purpose of Jesus coming and of the writing of the Gospel. The purpose of Jesus is to invite us into trust and mutual love, summed up in that picture of mutual abiding. The purpose of John's Gospel is to pass on the invitation. But there are powerful forces that resist such trust and love. Not only the invitation but also those who offer it and live in its light can be rejected. The result is the drama of the life, death and resurrection of Jesus and the ongoing drama that still continues. As we discussed in the introduction, *there can be no forcing true trust and love, and desires can go radically wrong.*

In face of rejection, Jesus' question reveals his own vulnerability. They are all free to reject him. And, as the glance forward (6:70–71) at his betrayal by Judas makes clear, there is worse to come.

Lent and desire in our culture

So, Jesus is about desire, and his life, death and resurrection are a drama of desire. This connects in the deepest way with life now as it did with life then.

This chapter opened with reflections on how much of human life is concerned with desire, and how our culture in particular is saturated with stimuli to desire through many media. It is worth thinking further about this and its connection with Lent.

Our family is, for most of us, the first place where our desires are expressed and formed in interaction with the desires of parents, siblings and others. The quality of the attachments formed during our early years has profound long-term effects on our social, emotional and learning development. Inadequate relationships, or childhoods dominated by insecurity, anxiety, lack of loving attention, suppression of normal feelings and desires, or some sort of overwhelming trauma can all cause lifelong problems.

I asked my daughter Rachel, who is a psychotherapist in a team that works on bonding between children in their early years and their parents, what top three things she most tries to enable. She said mutual attachment in trust; attunement to the desires, emotions and needs of the child; and play. We are all shaped complexly by our early years, and as parents, grandparents, teachers or others involved in forming children, we can carry over the healthy and unhealthy things from our own upbringing. Repairing inadequate or harmful patterns in these areas is one of the great challenges in any family – or society or church.

The education and re-education of our desires continues through life. It is worth reflecting regularly on how desire enters into our daily habits and patterns, our eating and drinking, our learning and knowing, our ways of getting and spending money, our entertainment and media use, our political and other commitments, our friendships and love life, our relationship with God – indeed, every significant area of life.

The forty days of Lent is a time when Christians are encouraged especially to focus on our desire for God in relation to other desires, all within the embracing desire of God for us and our flourishing. How can our response to the overwhelming love of God be enriched and help to shape lives, cultures and communities more fully?

Key biblical texts for Lent have always included the accounts of the forty days Jesus spent fasting in the wilderness after his baptism by John the Baptist. There, he was tempted through his desires for food, power and the impact he could have through a spectacular sign. John's Gospel does not tell of the temptations of Jesus in the wilderness that are described in the Gospels of Matthew and Luke as a conflict between Jesus and Satan. But the substance of the temptations parallels the conflict between the desires of Jesus and the desires of the crowd in John 6 that have been discussed above:

- Food: 'command this stone to become a loaf of bread' (Luke 4:2–4; see also Matthew 4:2–4).
- Power: authority over 'all the kingdoms of the world' (Luke 4:5–8; see also Matthew 4:8–10).
- A spectacular sign: 'throw yourself down' from the pinnacle of the Temple (Luke 4:9–12; see also Matthew 4:5–7).

Yet, besides the substance of the temptations, there is something even deeper in common: who Jesus is. Satan repeatedly makes the core identity of Jesus the issue: 'If you are the Son of God' (Luke 4:3, 9; Matthew 4:3, 6). The temptations immediately follow the baptism of Jesus, in which this core identity as 'the Son of God' has been dramatically affirmed: 'And a voice from heaven said, "This is my Son, the Beloved, with whom I am well pleased"' (Matthew 3:17; Luke 3:22). John draws readers even deeper into who Jesus is and especially into this relationship between Jesus and his Father, with John 6 a major step on the way.

As we will see – and as those who are taking part in the practice suggested at the beginning of this book should have begun to experience – the greatest depths are opened up in the prayer of Jesus in John 17. That will be explored further in the coming chapters. But for now, given this chapter's theme, we note how that prayer of Jesus is an outpouring of his ultimate desire to his Father at the most important time of his life. And at its climax in 17:20–26, as he prays for all of us who have come to follow him since that time, that we – and the whole world – might enter fully into the intensity of life, glory and love that he shares with his Father, he can simply say, 'Father, I desire' (17:24).

Questions for individual reflection and group discussion

Suggested by Revd Canon Amiel Osmaston.

1 At the start of chapter 3, we read, 'A huge amount of our personal lives and our culture is about desire. Life is full of choices, decisions, hopes, fears, things we want and things we don't want …' How does our society and consumer culture shape and pressurise us to desire? What should we do about it?

2 David Ford writes, 'The purpose of the whole Gospel and each of its chapters is to draw us deeper and deeper into this drama of desire, inspiring us to devote ourselves more and more to desires that are in tune with the desires of Jesus.' What are we most deeply desiring and looking for, as individuals and/or as a church? Is it in tune with the desires of Jesus?

3 In the story of Jesus feeding the five thousand, David contrasts the crowd's desire for power, food and signs with the desire for Jesus and the life he gives. Are we truly 'looking for Jesus', desiring to come closer to him, hungry to receive from him in our everyday lives? What has most helped you in doing this?

4 David writes, 'Repairing inadequate or harmful patterns [of desire] … is one of the great challenges in any family – or society, or church … The education and re-education of our desires continues through life … The forty days of Lent is a time when Christians are encouraged especially to focus on our desire for

God in relation to other desires, all within the embracing desire of God for us and our flourishing.' How can our response to the overwhelming love of God be enriched and help to shape lives, cultures and communities more fully?

4

Home: 'Where are you staying?'

The first words of the first disciples of Jesus, responding to his question asking what they are looking for, are '"Rabbi" (which translated means Teacher), "Where are you staying?"' (John 1:38).

The Greek word translated 'staying' is *menein*, and it is a key word in John's Gospel. Besides 'stay', *menein* means 'abide, live, dwell, remain, have a place, endure, continue, last'. It is about life in the long term. In this Gospel, it is above all about life with God and in God, what is called 'eternal life' – the deep, lasting, love-inspired life that Jesus invites us into on both sides of death.

Meeting God can happen in very many ways, as many as there are people. Jesus calls each by name (10:3) and engages each of us with full understanding of who we are, what we desire and where we can be most completely at home – in the best sense of 'home', that is, where we can trust that we are loved and free to love. But will our response be to trust him? *If the encounter, however it happens, does lead us to trust him, that can be the beginning of what John calls* me-nein: *abiding, long-term living in trust and mutual love.*

The aim of John's Gospel is to attract readers into this permanent relationship. It can be described in many ways, such as receiving Jesus, following Jesus, believing and trusting in Jesus, loving Jesus and abiding in Jesus. The most explicit statement of the Gospel's ultimate aim is given in a direct address to us readers: 'that through believing and trusting you may have life in his name' (20:31).

True home

That opening question of the first disciples to Jesus, 'Where are you staying?', has an ordinary meaning. It leads them to go and see 'where he was staying [*menein*], and they remained [*menein*] with him that day' (1:39). The importance of *menein* and the 'where' question about Jesus is emphasised by the repetitions. Then, as the Gospel unfolds, other levels of meaning open up, and later in this chapter, we will concentrate on the parable of the vine. There, *menein* occurs eleven times in seventeen verses and leads us into mutual indwelling, which is at the heart of living as disciples of Jesus: 'Abide in me as I abide in you' (15:4). *That is where we can be most truly, deeply and lastingly at home.*

It is worth thinking for a while about what 'home' means to us. Place can be very important. Where do I feel most at home? What room, house or flat, garden or countryside? What village, town, city or country? Even more important are people. With whom do I feel most at home? Who can be trusted most? With whom do I share meals regularly? With whom do I frequently share confidences or make myself vulnerable to rejection or letdown? Who tells me 'home truths'? Among whom am I recognised, known, familiar? With whom do I have long-term relationships? Who is in my 'community of the heart'? When I am getting to know someone new and I am asked where my roots are, what do I say?

People have extraordinarily diverse ideas and experiences of home. Let us reflect on our own experiences of home and family in the past and right now – good, bad or mixed – and be open to what John's Gospel might mean for us.

For those first disciples meeting Jesus for the first time, where Jesus is staying means 'some place nearby' that he can invite them to 'come and see' (1:39). But for readers of the Prologue, a deeper level of where Jesus is and where our true home is has already been opened up.

Birth into a family beyond our natural family is this Gospel's first picture of what readers are being invited into: 'to all who received him, who believed [trusted and had faith] in his name, he gave power to become children of God, who were born, not of blood or of the will of the flesh or of the will of man, but of God' (1:12–13). That extraordinary family, sharing in God's own life, is then seen as a place of glory, truth and superabundant 'grace upon grace' (1:14–16).

Then, in the climactic headline statement of the Prologue, the deepest open secret of the family home is revealed. This is nothing less than the family-like relationship of love that we can trust is at the heart of all reality: 'No one has ever seen God. It is God the only Son, who is close to the Father's heart [literally, 'into the bosom of the Father'], who has made him known' (1:18). *This is the home life of utter love, from which the whole creation springs and into which, in the course of the Gospel, all readers are invited.* The author wants all their readers to know this love, as suggested by that vivid image of Jesus being in the bosom of the Father.

Later, 'the disciple whom Jesus loved', the Beloved Disciple, is dramatically introduced for the first time at the Last Supper reclining on the bosom or breast of Jesus (13:21–30). Then, at the very end of the story, just before the Beloved Disciple is credited with the testimony written in this Gospel, we are reminded of him reclining on the breast of Jesus (21:20).

The Beloved Disciple is in many ways a model of discipleship in this Gospel. He is never named, most likely because his love-centred identity is one that his message invites all his readers to share. The Beloved Disciple can be any of us. He is trusted and trusting, beloved and loving. In a moving event in John's account of the crucifixion,[1] he and the mother of Jesus (also anonymous in this Gospel, I suspect for the same reason – that we are all invited to identify with her[2]) are entrusted with each other in a new family life initiated by Jesus:

> Meanwhile, standing near the cross of Jesus were his mother, and his mother's sister, Mary the wife of Clopas, and Mary Magdalene. When Jesus saw his mother and the disciple whom he loved standing beside her, he said to his mother, 'Woman, here is your son.' Then he said to the disciple, 'Here is your

mother.' And from that hour the disciple took her into his own home.
(John 19:25–27)

That both affirms the 'natural' family and at the same time transforms it. This is true home. There is the deep love of mother for child and of disciple for teacher, friend for friend, brought together and taken up into a new household inspired by Jesus and his love for his mother and his disciple and friend. As he is bringing them together in this new way, Jesus is completing the laying down of his life that he has described as 'no one has greater love than this' (15:13). *This is a true home of unsurpassable love.*

The very last scene of the Gospel not only reminds readers of the Beloved Disciple on the breast of Jesus at the Last Supper but also emphasises *menein* yet again. Jesus says to Peter about the Beloved Disciple, 'If it is my will [and desire] that he remain [or abide (*menein*)] until I come, what is that to you?' (21:22; see also 21:23). Where are we to imagine the disciple abiding? In that 'true home' with the mother of Jesus, brought together by the love of Jesus as he suffers on the cross. That is the home where this Gospel was conceived: 'This is the disciple who is testifying to these things and has written them, and we know that his testimony is true' (21:24). And the crucified and resurrected Jesus has gone on forming homes of many sorts, through this Gospel, century after century and round the world – including in today's Lent groups! That mysterious 'we' who 'know that his testimony is true' can now include us.

A golden thread

The themes of abiding and home run like a golden thread through John's Gospel. We have so far focused mainly on the striking images of Jesus close to the heart of his Father, of the Beloved Disciple close to the heart of Jesus, and of the new household of the Beloved

Disciple and the mother of Jesus. *The Gospel is written to attract readers into that succession of mutual love: the Father with Jesus, Jesus with the Beloved Disciple and his mother, and now us, with all of them.*

Before going further into the parable of the vine (or vineyard), it is worth noting just a few of the many other ways our true home can be imagined.

In John 2:13–25, Jesus makes a startling family connection. First, he calls the Temple, with its rich, multidimensional history and immense religious and theological significance, 'my Father's house', his family home. Then, the Temple is astonishingly identified with his own body. It is an early hint at Jesus himself as the 'place' of dwelling. As our previous chapter on desire explored, this is made clear for the first time in John 6, where our hunger and thirst for deep and lasting life is fulfilled as mutual indwelling: 'Those who eat my flesh and drink my blood abide in me, and I in them' (6:56). The parable of the vine will deepen this further in terms of love, meaning and the 'I am' of Jesus.

In John 8, Jesus says that to know and trust him and what he says is to have a new home. Within it, each of us can be fully free – like a family member rather than a household slave:

If you continue [*menein*] in my word, you are truly my disciples; and you will know the truth, and the truth will make you free ... Very truly, I tell you, everyone who commits sin is a slave of sin. The slave does not have a permanent place in the household; the son has a place there [*menein*] forever. So if the Son makes you free, you will be free indeed.
(John 8:31–36)

But this golden thread of home and family life is not only seen through images and metaphors. In John 11, the climactic, most dramatic sign Jesus performs in his public ministry when he resuscitates the dead Lazarus involves an actual, literal, natural family. In the Gospel of John, Lazarus is the first person who is said to be loved by Jesus: 'Lord, he whom you love is ill' (11:3); 'See how he loved him!' (11:36). Lazarus and his sisters Martha and Mary are clearly close friends of Jesus – 'Jesus loved Martha and her sister and Lazarus' (11:5) – and the intensity of feeling that he reveals is striking: 'he was greatly disturbed in spirit and deeply moved … Jesus began to weep' (11:33–35). The intensity is mutual, as seen above all in the next chapter when Jesus is at a family meal and 'Mary took a pound of costly perfume made of pure nard, anointed Jesus' feet, and wiped them with her hair' (12:3).

I agree with those interpreters who see John describing here a model community of friends of Jesus alongside the picture of discipleship painted in the Farewell Discourses and the new household of the Beloved Disciple and the mother of Jesus.[3] When 'the house was filled with the fragrance of the perfume' (12:3), the scent turns this family home into an attractive, Jesus-centred sign of abundance and love.

Now for one more jewel on this golden thread before the parable of the vine. John 14 opens with Jesus saying:

> Do not let your hearts be troubled. Believe [and trust] in God, believe [and trust] also in me. In my Father's house there are many dwelling places [*monai,* derived from the verb *menein*]. If it were not so, would I have told you that I go to prepare a place for you? And if I go and prepare a place for you, I will come again and will take you to myself, so that where I am, there you may be also.
> (John 14:1–3)

This is the ultimate promise of a home on both sides of death. *It is a 'where' inseparable from a 'who'*: 'where I am, there you may be also'. This inseparability is immediately repeated after Thomas asks,

'Lord, we do not know where you are going. How can we know the way?' (14:5). Jesus says, 'I am the way, and the truth, and the life' (14:6). And that leads on into three fundamental statements by Jesus on indwelling. These prepare the way for engaging with the parable of the vine (to follow below in this chapter) and with the prayer of Jesus in John 17 (in the next chapter, on 'Glory: Meeting God in John'). The three statements are:

1 There is the gift of the Holy Spirit 'to be with you forever', about whom Jesus says that 'he abides [*menein*] with you, and he will be in you' (14:16–17).
2 Jesus promises, 'On that day you will know that I am in my Father, and you in me, and I in you' (14:20).
3 Jesus says, 'Those who love me will keep my word, and my Father will love them, and we will come to them and make our home [*monēn*, derived from the verb *menein*] with them' (14:23).

Put those together and we have an astonishing, mind-blowing reality: ourselves as utterly and for ever at home, beloved and loving, with the Holy Spirit, the Father and Jesus.[4] Let us now turn to the parable of the vine or vineyard.

The parable of the vine

John 15:1–17 is the centrepiece of the teaching of Jesus in chapters 13–16, which include his most substantial teaching in John's Gospel. It is extraordinarily rich, and we will return to it in later chapters of this book. For now, the key thing in it is the concentration on *menein* and the ways in which Jesus and those who trust and love him abide in each other. It deepens and expands what 'true home' means.

I suggest that you slowly read John 15:1–17. Enter into the meaning by imagining the relationships of Jesus, his Father and his followers through the vine and vineyard imagery. But also note the way in which the text, especially after verse 8, repeatedly points beyond the imagery to 'the word that I have spoken to you' (15:3), to prayer, love, commandments, joy and friendship. John is a teacher who goes to great lengths to make sure that readers get the message that there is always more and more meaning in his pictures and images – even if it can take a lifetime for any of us to plumb those depths.

Who to who: The dynamics of mutual indwelling

Meeting God through this parable draws readers into the dynamics of mutual indwelling. This has many dimensions, and it is one of the richest and most fascinating themes in Christian understanding and experience. I will highlight three elements that are in dynamic interaction: 'I am', 'my words' and 'my love'. I will not say much about them, but I will offer a few pointers that might be of help in personal reflection and group discussion.

1 'I am'

'I am', as we have seen in chapter 2 on 'Identity: "Who are you?"', is the most distinctive mark of the unique identity of Jesus, who is at one with the God who is revealed to Moses in Exodus 3:14 as Yahweh, 'I AM WHO I AM'. *The reality of our situation right now, wherever we are, is that Jesus is present with us as God is present.*

How can we begin to respond adequately to this infinitely amazing truth? The following two pointers open up practical ways to enter more and more fully into it and to live it day by day – in other words, to abide in this vine. Both pointers are rooted in who God is and in how Jesus has already taken the initiative in relating to us: 'You did not choose me but I chose you' (15:16). That is an initiative, as the Prologue has headlined, of the deepest meaning and the deepest love together.

2 'If you abide in me, and my words abide in you'

'If you abide in me, and my words abide in you' (15:7). This is a vital clue to the daily reality of abiding. *We are to have the words of Jesus abiding in us.* How does that happen?

First of all, obviously, it happens by hearing or reading the words and trusting them. A first reading or hearing is like an initial meeting, but to abide in Jesus is to continually re-hear and reread them. It is to 'read, mark, learn and inwardly digest' them (as a classic prayer about reading the Bible says); to savour them repeatedly; to study them and ask questions about them; to connect them with other deep meaning in the Scriptures, hymns, liturgies, literature and the arts, the media and many other sources; to see them in our own life experiences; and to let the words of Jesus and who Jesus is shape who we are and what we desire.

The connection that Jesus makes at once is with our desires and our relationship with God in prayer: 'ask for whatever you wish/desire, and it will be done for you' (15:7). We will go deeper into prayer and into that stupendous promise in later chapters.

As you try to take in what it might mean to have 'my words abide in you', begin right here with the parable of the vine and learn from one another. Remember that all these words of Jesus are addressed to 'you' in the plural – the words are to 'abide in' us as a family group and community at home with him. Share the meaning you find with one another.

3 'Abide in my love'

'As the Father has loved me, so I have loved you; abide in my love' (15:9). What is 'abide in my love'? An invitation? A call? A command? A desire? A promise? A heartfelt cry? A passionate appeal? In the context of the rest of the Gospel, it is all those together. It is rooted in the ultimate good news: 'As the Father has loved me, so I have loved you'. *It is the greatest challenge any of us ever faces: to receive this, trust this and live this.* It usually happens in waves (which is

51

probably why John's Gospel often teaches in waves). We may receive it – after who knows what twists and turns in our lives and thoughts and imaginations! – tentatively or wholeheartedly. Then we may find that there is so much more than, or different from, what we first expected. Meeting God through this Gospel is one thing; maturing in our trusting, understanding, praying and loving is another. John's Gospel, as we have found, is about both the meeting and the maturing. *At the heart of both is the mutuality of love.*

This is why our response is insisted upon: 'If you keep my commandments, you will abide in my love, just as I have kept my Father's commandments and abide in his love' (15:10). That leads into the second great wave of what Jesus teaches on love in these Farewell Discourses. The first wave, in John 13, connected the new commandment of love with the humble service of having just washed the feet of his disciples. Here, without at all weakening that imperative of loving service, *the emphasis is on the fuller mutuality of friendship.* That includes mutual knowledge and understanding and even the willingness to lay down our lives (15:12–17). We can abide in the love of someone whose friendship embraces us on both sides of death. His words that abide in us include, 'I am the resurrection and the life' (11:25). And, because of that death-conquering and love-filled life, his words also include, 'I have said these things to you so that my joy may be in you, and that your joy may be complete' (15:11).

Yet more

If we are to receive, trust and live this parable and the gift of friendship with Jesus that follows from it, there is one massive, repeated imperative: 'This is my commandment, that you love one another as I have loved you' (15:12). It is the more-than-necessity of Christian community. What might that mean for us now? What is our way of belonging to the Church? What about the local, regional, national and international dimensions of that? How are we bound to other Christians? How are we divided from them? What might be the practical implications of the 'as' in 'love one another *as* I have loved you'? How has Jesus loved? How was and is he a friend? How can the daring and deep friendships of Jesus – with the Samaritan woman at the well, with Martha, Mary and Lazarus, with Mary Magdalene, with Peter, with the Beloved Disciple – inspire us?

John 15:1–17 is in many ways a peak in the teaching of Jesus in chapters 13–16. Yet there is an even higher summit to come in the prayer of Jesus in John 17, as will be seen in the next chapter, 'Glory: Meeting God in John'. But for now, we can seek to let the words of John 15 abide in us and, inspired by them, desire to abide more fully in the love of Jesus as our friend and in the love of his other friends here and around the world.

Questions for individual reflection and group discussion

Suggested by Revd Canon Amiel Osmaston.

1 Where are your roots? Where do you belong? Where feels like 'home' for you? How do you think this has shaped you?

2 Reflecting on John 14, David Ford concludes, 'We have an aston-ishing, mind-blowing reality: ourselves as utterly and for ever at home, beloved and loving, with the Holy Spirit, the Father and Jesus.' Do you feel equally 'at home' with all three members of the Trinity: the Holy Spirit, the Father and Jesus? Does this affect how you pray and how you envisage God's presence with you?

3 Jesus says, 'If you abide in me and my words abide in you' (John 15:7) and, 'As the Father has loved me, so I have loved you; abide in my love' (15:9). How can we / do we 'abide in Jesus'? What has most helped you to do this? How has your church helped you to do this?

4 Is there anything in this chapter which has helped (or could help) you and others to feel more confident and peaceful in the face of death?

5

Glory: Meeting God in John

To meet God in John is to meet the glory of God in Jesus. The testimony of John's Gospel is clear: 'And the Word became flesh and lived among us, and we have seen his glory, the glory as of a father's only son,[1] full of grace and truth' (John 1:14).

One way to meet the glory of God in Jesus now is to trust the testimony of John. When Thomas sees the crucified and resurrected Jesus and realises that he is meeting God, he cries out, 'My Lord and my God!' (20:28). Then, Jesus says, 'Have you believed and trusted because you have seen me? Blessed are those who have not seen and yet have come to believe and trust' (20:29). Immediately, John goes on to address his readers and sum up the purpose of his Gospel, which is 'written so that you may come to believe and trust that Jesus is the Messiah, the Son of God, and that through believing and trusting you may have life in his name' (20:31). The readers can be blessed without seeing for themselves.

We have been following this way of meeting God through reading John, and in this chapter will continue to do so through John's key term: 'glory'. As we will see, *glory is John's main way to the heart of God's life and to the heart of a life of trusting and loving God.*

What is glory? Some stretching exercises

Glory can mean many things and has many associations. To prepare the muscles of our imaginations, minds and hearts for what follows in this chapter, I offer a few stretching exercises:

- As always in John's Gospel, ask first about 'who' more than 'what'. Think of the people, past and present, in whom you have glimpsed the sort of glory you can admire wholeheartedly. You might try the 'fruit of the Spirit' checklist: love, joy, peace and peacemaking, patience, kindness and generosity, goodness, faith and trust, faithfulness and trustworthiness, gentleness and humility, and self-control. Who shines with some of these?
- St Irenaeus said, 'The glory of God is a human being fully alive.' That can be extended to a friendship, a family or a community full of life and love. Where have you glimpsed that?
- There is something overwhelming, overflowing and 'over the top' about God's glory. For me, a word that goes well with it is 'utterly'. Utterly wonderful. Utterly amazing. Utterly surprising. Utterly liberating. Utterly inspiring. Utterly rapturous. Utterly beautiful. Utterly graceful. Utterly good. Utterly real. Utterly true. Utterly reliable. Utterly radiant. Utterly worth praising.[2] Utterly and infinitely glorious! How have you experienced hints or signs of anything like those?
- The radiant face is one of the greatest images of glory. Paul wrote, 'For it is the God who said, "Let light shine out of darkness," who has shone in our hearts to give the light of the knowledge of the glory of God in the face of Jesus Christ' (2 Corinthians 4:6). Many other glory texts in the Bible involve faces. And one of the most moving and delightful ways of imagining glory is through smiling. The New Living Translation even translates Psalm 67:1, 'May God be merciful and bless us. May his face smile with favour on us.'[3]

That brings us to the glory-centred stretching exercise done daily by millions of Jews and Christians: praying – and often singing – the Psalms. Try it!

Why glory?

In the Prologue (which is always worth rereading alongside every chapter of John and in relation to each leading theme), the glory of Jesus is understood as abundant 'grace and truth'. And this glory is also 'as of a father's only son', which points forward to the culminating verse: 'No one has seen God. It is God the only Son, who is close to the Father's heart, who has made him known' (John 1:18). We have already begun to explore this, the divine love that is the core reality into which readers of this Gospel are being invited. This love, embodied in Jesus, is the deepest secret of the identity and desire of his followers, where they can be fully at home, abiding in his love – 'beloved'.

One lesson of the Prologue and the rest of John's Gospel is that love and glory are utterly inseparable.[4] Yet it is striking that the Prologue headlines glory and light but does not mention love explicitly. Indeed, for the first twelve chapters of John's Gospel, glory (as we will see) is a framing reality, and while love occurs at important points (read 3:16, 29, 35; 5:20; 10:17; 11:3, 5, 11, 36) glory's main companion terms are 'life' and 'light' rather than love. This changes in the Farewell Discourses, whose framing reality (as we will see) is still glory but now inseparable from love. Then, in the final chapter, love and glory come together again. The love between Peter and Jesus is repeatedly affirmed, and Jesus indicates 'the kind of death by which he [Peter] would glorify God' (21:19). So, looking at the Gospel as a whole, the main consistent and framing reality, beginning with the Prologue, is glory. Why?

There is a clear, obvious, vitally important answer to the question, 'Why glory?' The answer is, 'God!'

John is a God-centred Gospel. The first clue is there in the Prologue, beginning with its first verse: 'In the beginning was the Word, and the Word was with God, and the Word was God' (1:1). Through the rest of the Gospel, Jesus, as the human self-expression and self-giving of God, is the 'I am' at one with God, from God, with God, sent by God, the only Son of God, the Lamb of God and more. Jesus repeatedly refers to his Father, and his identity is united with that of his Father – 'The Father and I are one' (10:30) – so to be centred on Jesus is also to be centred on God.

Glory can be used in relation to people, but above all it is God related.

John is steeped in the Psalms. Through glorifying, praising, honouring, blessing, magnifying, thanking, exalting and more, they are supremely focused on God and God's glory, or closely related qualities and actions – God's majesty, radiance, shining face, love, wisdom, compassion, justice and glorious creation.

The Temple is above all the place of God's glory in Israel. John has far more about the Temple and its festivals than any other Gospel. Early in his narrative, he identifies the Temple with the body of Jesus (2:21) about whom the Prologue has already said, 'We have seen his glory' (1:14).

Through chapter after chapter, the centrality of God and God's initiative emerges again and again even apart from the theme of glory: 'God so loved the world' (3:16); 'the Father seeks such as these to worship him' (4:23); 'My Father is still working ... the Father raises the dead ... the Father has life in himself' (5:17, 21, 26); 'it is on him that God the Father has set his seal ... I have come down from heaven, not to do my own will [and desire], but the will [and desire] of him who sent me ... No one can come to me unless drawn by the Father who sent me' (6:27, 38, 44); 'I know him, because I am from him, and he sent me' (7:29); 'the Father who sent me testifies on my behalf ... I speak these things as the Father instructed me' (8:18, 28); 'If this man were not from God he could do nothing' (9:33); 'For this reason the Father loves me ... The works that I do in my Father's name testify to me ... What my Father has given me is greater than all else, and no one can snatch it out of the Father's hand. The Father and I are one ... the Father is in me and I am in the Father' (10:17, 25, 29–30, 38);

'it is for God's glory ... Did I not tell you that if you believed you would see the glory of God?' (11:4, 40).

Such verses are worth meditating on one by one, and there are many more to be noted in reading later chapters. I have stopped at John 11 in preparation for opening up, below, the extraordinary focus on God and God's glory in John 12, and then, even more fully, in the prayer of Jesus in chapter 17. The accumulation of passages through John is overwhelming in its affirmation of God.

The better-known passages in John's Gospel tend to be centred on Jesus (3:16 is a partial exception), so it is all the more important to be reminded of the utter God-centredness of Jesus and of this Gospel. This God is the central, embracing and comprehensive reality for Jesus, for John, for the rest of the New Testament and for their Scriptures – Israel's Scriptures.

The supreme truth is the one, living, glorious, holy, wise, compassionate, loving God, and all reality in relationship with this God. The supreme message, commandment, invitation and shaper of identity, desire and the whole of life is given in the cry of Deuteronomy: 'Hear, O Israel: the Lord is our God, the Lord alone. You shall love the Lord your God with all your heart, and with all your soul, and with all your might' (Deuteronomy 6:4–5). *Any thought of identity, desire or home life needs to give priority to that.* Indeed, Deuteronomy immediately goes on to say how completely every day and night of our lives – our inner and outer lives, and all our relationships – needs to be soaked in this truth, this reality, this love: 'Keep these words that I am commanding you today in your heart. Recite them to your children and talk about them when you are at home and when you are away, when you lie down and when you rise' (Deuteronomy 6:6–7). And Jesus, in the Gospel of Matthew, says:

> 'You shall love the Lord your God with all your heart, and with all your soul, and with all your mind.' This is the greatest and first commandment. And a second is like it: 'You shall love your

neighbour as yourself.' On these two commandments hang all the law and the prophets.
(Matthew 22:38–40)[5]

There can be no greater priority than this double love command. When, for example, Jesus teaches his disciples to pray in what has come to be known as the Lord's Prayer – 'Your kingdom come, your will [and desire] be done, on earth as it is in heaven' (Matthew 6:10) – it is love of God and love of neighbour that we are to think of as God's desire. That is our guide in all interpretation of the Scriptures.[6]

The Gospel of John is in line with all that, and it goes even further and deeper. Our Lent exercise has been to pray the Lord's Prayer in the light of the prayer of Jesus in John 17. There, *the desire of Jesus is for utter unity, in glory, truth and love, with God and with one another for the sake of the whole world*. That is a way of imagining the fulfilment of the double love command and the Kingdom of God. And, astonishingly, it involves receiving the very glory that Jesus and his Father share: 'The glory that you have given me I have given them, so that they may be one, as we are one' (John 17:22). We will now try to go deeper into what that glory means in John's Gospel.

Glory in John: Signs of abundant life for all

After the Prologue's headline, 'We have seen his glory' (1:14), and its source in the divine love, 'God the only Son, who is close to the Father's heart' (1:18), the life-shaping questions in the rest of John 1 help to form the community of those who, through trusting Jesus, share in that glory and love. I have taken those questions as the way into the whole Gospel during Lent. They are so important, deep and endlessly generative that they are worth asking daily through the year:

- *'Who are you?'* Who is God? Who is Jesus? Who are we? Who am I?
- *'What are you looking for?'* What and whom do we – do I – desire?
- *'Where are you staying?'* Where are we – am I – at home? With whom? With what sort of commitment?

Immediately after the gathering of this community of learners in John 1, they are all invited to a wedding together with the mother of Jesus (2:1–12). What happens there is summed up as 'Jesus did this, the first of his signs, in Cana of Galilee, and revealed his glory, and his disciples [or learners] believed and trusted in him' (2:11).

That suggests why John, unique among the Gospels, tells this story and even makes it the first of what he calls the 'signs' that Jesus does in his public ministry. The glory of Jesus is here seen at a wedding, signifying celebration, love, joy and a new family life. There is a crisis in the celebration when the wine runs out. The mother of Jesus appeals to him, and Jesus (so quietly that no one except his mother, his disciples and the servants who drew the water seem aware of what has happened) does more than just solve the problem of not enough wine; he turns a huge amount of water into a superabundance of the best wine: 'six stone water jars ... each holding twenty or thirty gallons ... "You have kept the good wine until now"' (2:6–10). *The glory of Jesus is revealed in a quiet way that only a few connect with him, but many receive the benefit.*

The signal phrase 'the first of his signs' encourages us to look for more signs revealing more glory. We find one after another in his public ministry. The second is in chapter 4. A royal official begs Jesus to heal his son, and quietly, without even going to the boy, Jesus says, 'Go, your son will live' (4:50). The boy recovers, and the official 'believed [trusted and had faith], along with his whole household' (4:53). Jesus goes on doing signs: healing, feeding and then, in his climactic public sign, bringing his dead friend Lazarus back to life, about which he says, 'Did I not tell you that if you believed, you would see the glory of God?' (11:40).

What has been happening through these signs in chapters 2–11? *They have been revealing the glory of Jesus, and of God, through signs of abundant life for all.* Jesus responds to human needs in love and service. They might lead to some people believing, trusting and committing to him, but they seem to be done above all because they are needed, because they do not benefit only those who believe and because they often have that quality of overflowing superabundance that is so characteristic of the glory of God. *This is not just problem-solving or meeting needs, though it is that; it is new, glorious, more-than-satisfying life beyond anything that could be deserved, expected or even imagined.* All the five thousand are fed, but that is not all: 'When they were satisfied, he told his disciples, "Gather up the fragments left over, so that nothing may be lost." So they gathered them up, and from the fragments of the five barley loaves, left by those who had eaten, they filled twelve baskets' (6:12–13). The man born blind not only receives his sight, but also someone new in his life whom he can trust completely (9:38). In the very first sign, all the guests at the wedding enjoy wine that is more abundant and of higher quality than anything needed to meet the crisis. Richard Wilbur's superb poem 'A Wedding Toast' says it beautifully:

It made no earthly sense, unless to show
How whatsoever love elects to bless
Brims to a sweet excess
That can without depletion overflow.[7]

We will be discussing below the core vocation the resurrected Jesus gives his disciples when he breathes the Holy Spirit into them: 'As the Father has sent me, so I send you' (20:21; see also the prayer of Jesus, 17:18). *What signs of abundant life for all, within and beyond the Christian community, might his followers in the twenty-first century be sent to do?* What quiet, mostly unrecognised signs? What louder, public ones?

Preparing for the crucifixion of Jesus, the greatest sign of God's glory and love

The raising of Lazarus leads into John 12, where readers are prepared for the 'hour' – that is, the climax of the drama in the Last Supper, the arrest, trial and crucifixion of Jesus, and his resurrection. At the wedding in Cana, Jesus said to his mother, 'My hour has not yet come' (2:4). Now, in chapter 12, it has.

First comes the only sign that is done to Jesus rather than by Jesus – when Mary anoints Jesus' feet with costly perfume and wipes them with her hair, and Jesus sees this as pointing to his burial. Then, Jesus enters Jerusalem on a donkey and is hailed as a king by 'the great crowd that had come to the festival' (12:12–13). After that, when some Greeks (who represent the rest of the world beyond Israel) come and ask to see Jesus, he makes the momentous announcement: 'The hour has come for the Son of Man to be glorified' (12:23).

As readers, we are being given three ways of preparing ourselves ahead of the uniquely important event of the crucifixion of Jesus. I suggest that you read 12:20–36, but concentrate mainly on the second preparation, 12:27–28, where God's glory is the focus.

The first preparation: Like a grain of wheat

The first preparation challenges us to trust Jesus, follow Jesus, be with Jesus, serve Jesus and love Jesus even more than our own lives:

> Very truly, I tell you, unless a grain of wheat falls into the earth and dies, it remains just a single grain; but if it dies, it bears much fruit. Those who love their life lose it, and those who hate their life in this world will keep it for eternal life.
> (John 12:24–26)

This profound, radical mystery is in line with the way creation works. Jesus himself is the one who above all realises and embodies this truth and produces abundant fruit. He is willing to lose his life for the sake of love – for the sake of the glory of the God of love with whom he is utterly identified. He shows that there is something and someone more important than our lives on this side of death. More acutely, he exposes how much in our world resists, rejects, opposes and even hates the life, light, truth and love that he embodies. There is what John has called, from the opening of his Gospel, 'darkness' (1:5). Such darkness (and its presence in the world, in each of us and in our communities – including the Church), together with its consequences in suffering, misery, sin, lies, injustice, destruction and death, is to be hated, resisted, rejected and opposed for the sake of life, light, truth, justice, joy and love. *So, life as we know it in our world is not all there is, not ultimate, not the last word about life.* We can even, like Jesus, give our lives for the sake of the deep, lasting, God-centred life of glory, love and joy that is called 'eternal life'. And eternal life is a reality on both sides of death, because it is embodied in Jesus, the 'I am' who is present as God is present, breathing out his Spirit freely. As we will see in chapter 8 on Good Friday, it is very important that John describes Jesus, in dying, as handing over the s/Spirit (19:30).

This first preparation for the death of Jesus confronts anyone ('whoever') who encounters him with a strong, unavoidable 'must'. *To meet Jesus 'very truly' is to be called to entrust your whole self, life and future to him and, inseparably, to 'the Father'*: 'Whoever serves me must follow me, and where I am, there will my servant be also. Whoever serves me, the Father will honour' (12:26). That reads like a summary of answers to the three core questions about identity, desire and home, and the promise of divine honouring opens into this chapter's subject of glory.

The third preparation: Ultimate attraction

The third way of preparing readers to take in what the death of Jesus means, which is mind-blowing in its all-embracing promise:

'Now is the judgement of this world; now the ruler of this world will be driven out. And I, when I am lifted up from the earth, will draw all people [according to some ancient manuscripts, 'all things', meaning all creation] to myself.' He said this to indicate the kind of death he was to die.
(John 12:31–33)

Jesus, through giving up his life by being lifted up on the cross, demonstrates the truth about our world, showing that its darkness does not win and that the ultimate power belongs to him and his light, life and love and not to whatever or whoever else might seem to dominate the world. But Jesus, through whom 'all things came into being' and in whom 'was life, and the life was the light of all people' (1:3–4), is also *the ultimate attractor*, the one through whom all of us can find our home, our deepest meaning, the fulfilment of our deepest desires, and our most life-giving relationships with God, with one another and with all creation.

The second, central preparation: Ultimate glory and love

But at the centre of this preparation for the dramatic, surprising climax in the crucifixion of Jesus is the second way in which John draws readers into its very heart, *the glory of God*:

'Now my soul is troubled. And what should I say – "Father, save me from this hour"? No, it is for this reason that I have come to this hour. Father, glorify your name.' Then a voice came from heaven, 'I have glorified it, and I will glorify it again.'
(John 12:27–28)

This is the only time the 'voice … from heaven', the voice of the Father, is heard in John, which underlines its immense, unique importance. In the other Gospels, this voice affirms Jesus in the two key events of his baptism and transfiguration. John refers to the baptism of Jesus, but does not tell of his transfiguration, which is the main event in which his glory is seen in Matthew, Mark and Luke. Instead, John sees the glory of Jesus in all his signs and framing the whole Gospel but above all, as here, in his crucifixion. Here, there are echoes not only of his transfiguration but also, in 'my soul is troubled', of his agony as he prays in the garden of Gethsemane, which is also not described by John (the prayer John concentrates on is at the Last Supper in John 17, to which we will come soon, and which opens with a burst of glory).

It is as if John is distilling into these two short verses the essence of what the other Gospels tell through the baptism, transfiguration and agonised Gethsemane prayer of Jesus as he approaches his crucifixion. Each of those events has at its centre the love relationship of Jesus with his Father (it is worth taking time to read and reflect on them together). Here, that love is concentrated in the desire of Jesus, 'Father, glorify your name'. *The essence is the love and glory of who God is. And the death of Jesus goes to the heart of who God is in love and glory. This above all is where we meet God.*

At once, the promise of this encounter is offered to readers: 'And I, when I am lifted up from the earth, will draw all people to myself' (12:32). The 'where' of meeting God is this 'who': 'I … I … myself.'

The summit of glory and love

The preparation for the crucifixion and resurrection of Jesus continues through the Farewell Discourses. They will be opened up further during the chapters of this book on Holy Week and beyond. They begin (13:31–32) and end (17:1–5, 22) with massive affirmations of glory as the intensity and scope of the divine life and love shared by Jesus and his Father are revealed and shared with us readers.

For now, as we think of ourselves (at least in imagination) as completing Lent and heading into Holy Week, let us enter again into the prayer of Jesus in John 17. If as a group you have been following the practice suggested for Lent and praying the Lord's Prayer in the light of John 17, you might want to share your experiences of that practice now. Then, as we move into Holy Week, I suggest rereading and meditating on John 17:20–26 as a preparation for the drama to come – both the drama of the passion, death and resurrection of Jesus and the ongoing drama of glory and love in our lives and communities. These verses invite us into the ultimate desire of Jesus for us, for all humanity and for all creation. *His desire, and promise, is nothing less than for us to be united in glory and love with him and his Father, and with each other, for the sake of the world God loves.*

I ask not only on behalf of these, but also on behalf of those who will believe in me through their word, that they may all be one. As you, Father, are in me and I am in you, may they also be in us, so that the world may believe that you have sent me. The glory that you have given me I have given them, so that they may be one, as we are one, I in them and you in me, that they may become completely one, so that the world may know that you have sent me and have loved them even as you have loved me. Father, I desire that those also, whom you have given me, may be with me where I am, to see my glory, which you have given me because you loved me before the foundation of the world.

'Righteous Father, the world does not know you, but I know you; and these know that you have sent me. I made your name known to them, and I will make it known, so that the love with which you have loved me may be in them, and I in them.'
(John 17:20–26)

*

This completes the part of this book that has been written with Lent groups in mind. These first five chapters have been imagined as complete in themselves, but the remaining chapters are written for those who want to go further with the Gospel of John as an accompaniment to Holy Week and, beyond that, into the Easter season and on to Ascension, Pentecost and Trinity Sunday.

Questions for individual reflection and group discussion

Suggested by Revd Canon Amiel Osmaston.

1 How can we even begin to imagine God's glory? How can we respond to the eternal, uncreated, awesome life of God in its infinite intensity and extensity of glory and love? Think of the Gloria in the Eucharist, or some of the Psalms, or great music, or the glory of creation, or the face of Jesus in icons of the transfiguration, or great poetry, or whatever or whoever inspires your wonder and admiration. What resonates for you? What has helped you to glimpse God's glory?

2 'The glory that you have given me I have given them, so that they may be one, as we are one' (John 17:22). In what ways have you seen something of the glory that Jesus has passed on to the community of his followers? Do you have any examples or experiences? How is the glory related to our unity?

3 Jesus performed 'signs' and said to his disciples, 'As the Father has sent me, so I send you' (20:21). David asks, 'What signs of abundant life for all, within and beyond the Christian community, might his followers in the twenty-first century be sent to do?' Can you think of any examples or suggestions?

4 Towards the end of chapter 5, David draws out some of the 'resonances' between John 17 and the Lord's Prayer. Which of these resonances or connections do you think might help you to pray the Lord's Prayer with even more depth and insight?

Part 2

THE HOUR
HAPPENS

'My hour has not yet come,' Jesus says to his mother before doing his first sign (John 2:4). The whole of the Gospel of John up to chapter 12, and the whole of Lent, can be understood as a preparation for the happening of that 'hour'.

In John 12, after dramatically riding a donkey into Jerusalem and being greeted by cheering crowds on the Sunday ('Palm Sunday') before Passover, Jesus makes the momentous announcement: 'The hour has come for the Son of Man to be glorified' (12:23). Then, he sounds the depths of his coming crucifixion in three ways, which we have opened up in the previous chapter.

There is more preparation in depth to come. In chapters 13 – 17 of John's Gospel, Jesus shares a final meal with his disciples. He prepares them for the grief they will soon experience, gives his longest single body of teaching and prays an extraordinary final prayer. We have opened up parts of this teaching and prayer in previous chapters (see especially chapter 4 on the parable of the vine in John 15; chapter 5 on glory, love and 17:20–26), and we have encouraged praying the Lord's Prayer in the light of John 17. We will enter further into John 13 – 17 in Part 3 on the ongoing drama of Christian living, because a great deal in these five chapters is oriented beyond the crucifixion and resurrection of Jesus.

But these five chapters have their own mealtime drama in John 13, closely related to the following events of the 'hour' when Jesus is arrested, tried, crucified and resurrected.

Part 2 of this book now focuses first, in chapter 6, on the events of John 13, especially on Jesus washing the feet of his disciples. This, together with the 'new commandment' of love that follows, gives the most basic imperative of Christian living. We will also ask about a mysterious omission. Why is there no mention of what the other three Gospels, and Paul in 1 Corinthians, describe: Jesus during his final meal initiating what has come to be called the Lord's Supper, Holy Communion, the Eucharist or the Mass? And in the dramatic exchanges of Jesus with his Beloved Disciple, Judas Iscariot and Peter, we will see the Gospel's core reality of mutual love alongside its betrayal and denial.

Next, in chapter 7, comes the arrest, trial, flogging, crucifixion and burial of Jesus, with an answer to a question that goes to the heart of Christian faith and life: 'What happens in the death of Jesus?'

That question could not be answered fully without referring to the resurrection of Jesus, the subject of our chapter 8. It is through the encounters of the risen Jesus with his followers in John 20 and 21 that we readers are invited into the depth, breadth, height and ongoing surprise of the reality of meeting God in John. Meeting God in John includes meeting the crucified and risen Jesus; Jesus as teacher, 'Rabbouni!' (20:16); God as Jesus' Father and ours; peace; joy; being sent as Jesus was sent; receiving the Holy Spirit; receiving and giving forgiveness; knowing Jesus as 'My Lord and my God!' (20:28); trusting the testimony of the Beloved Disciple; being asked by Jesus, 'Do you love me?' (21:15, 16, 17); facing the cost of following Jesus; seeing Jesus as the one sure reality in our future; and being open to the superabundance of further meaning and truth: 'I suppose that the world itself could not contain the books that would be written' (21:25).

6

Thursday: Loving utterly, intimately, vulnerably, mutually

'Having loved his own who were in the world, he loved them to the end' (John 13:1). That is the headline for the climactic evening of the life of Jesus, the evening before he died. His life, his death and his resurrection are about love. The first time the word 'love' is mentioned in the Gospel of John is when Jesus says, 'God so loved the world that he gave his only Son, so that everyone who believes [and trusts] in him may not perish but may have eternal life' (3:16) – that is, deep, lasting, God-given and love-filled life on both sides of death. Love sums up what that life is about.

In John 13, as Jesus approaches 'the end', his own death, he performs a profoundly important sign by washing the feet of his disciples. His crucifixion the next day will be the unique, one-off happening of love for the world (see our next chapter). This foot-washing points to the thing that is most essential for those who want to imitate his love in ordinary, everyday life with one another: loving, mutual service. The meaning of the foot-washing will be our main focus in John 13, but we will also say something about the rest of the chapter, both its massive omission and its demonstration of love and the ways love can fail.

The best preparation for what follows is to read the whole of John 13 slowly, and then reread 13:12–20.

A radical act

Immediately after announcing the love of Jesus as the headline for the 'hour', John makes three things clear about what is happening in this decisive time:

1 There is a powerful, deadly hostility to this love: 'The devil had already put it into the heart of Judas son of Simon Iscariot to betray him' (13:2).
2 The most important reality in these events is who Jesus is: the Son of God into whose 'hands' his Father has entrusted 'all things' and who 'had come from God and was going to God' (13:3). The utter unity of Jesus and his Father in trust, glory and love is opened up further in John 14–17, climaxing in his prayer: 'Father, glorify me in your own presence with the glory that I had in your presence before the world existed … my glory, which you have given me because you loved me before the foundation of the world' (17:5–24). What is happening now is rooted in the divine glory and love at the origin of the universe.
3 Glory and love are being given a radically new form and content by what is happening in this 'hour', beginning when Jesus 'got up from the table, took off his outer robe, and tied a towel around himself. Then he poured water into a basin and began to wash the disciples' feet' (13:4–5). *The first thing done by those hands, into which God has given all things, is to wash feet, a slave's job.*

This is the sort of thing God wants to be done. It scandalises Peter. Jesus then teaches its meaning.

The meaning

It is hard to overestimate how important this teaching in 13:12–20 is. It is happening at the most important of all times, the 'hour'.

It demonstrates the sort of love that is at the heart of the life, death and resurrection of Jesus, and it is a key to who Jesus is: 'You call me Teacher and Lord – and you are right, for that is what I am' (13:13).

Jesus puts his whole authority behind making it a strong command: 'So if I, your Lord and Teacher, have washed your feet, you also ought to wash one another's feet' (13:14). The mutuality of it, doing it to one another, means that it is key to healthy community. But Jesus is not just giving a command; he is also living it himself: 'For I have set you an example, that you also should do as I have done to you' (13:15).

That 'do as I have done' leads directly into the 'new commandment' later in the meal: 'Just as I have loved you, you also should love one another' (13:34). The 'do as I have done' not only puts loving service at the heart of Christian living, but it also encourages continual creativity in how we do it. Following an example does not mean doing exactly the same thing in all circumstances; it calls for thoughtfulness, discernment, imagination and taking into account all the elements in our situation. We ask, every day, 'How can the example of Jesus be followed today?' The 'as' becomes an encouragement to love and serve as wholeheartedly as Jesus did, continually improvising on his example and risking new initiatives as he did. This gives a new, surprising idea of who is great and important and what greatness is: 'Very truly, I tell you, servants are not greater than their master, nor are messengers greater than the one who sent them' (13:16).

What if the example of Jesus in service, done in love, were to be the measure of greatness in our culture, in politics or on social media? In the Church? In households and families? What are the challenges and the problems? There is even a beatitude, one of only two in the Gospel of John,[1] a promise to those who follow this command: 'If you know these things, you are blessed if you do them' (13:17).

There is realism about how this ethos of mutual love and service can be rejected, violated and betrayed, and about the potential cost of living it, for which the authority of the Scriptures is invoked:

'But it is to fulfil the scripture, "The one who ate my bread has lifted his heel against me"' (13:18). And to crown all this, there is even an invocation of the most important truth about Jesus – his divine identity, his 'I am' – and the most important, basic thing on our side, our trust in who he is: 'I tell you this now, before it occurs, so that when it does occur, you may believe [trust and have faith] that I am he' (13:19).

Yet, amazingly, that is not all. Perhaps the most astonishing statement of all is the final one, whose importance is brought home by repeating the 'very truly' that has already been used to emphasise who and what is truly great: 'Very truly, I tell you, whoever receives one whom I send receives me; and whoever receives me receives him who sent me' (13:20). *That is about nothing less than meeting God!*

What has happened? Jesus – Teacher and Lord, in the most important 'hour' of his life – has done the tender, touching, loving act of washing the feet of his disciples (soon, in 15:15, he will also call them his 'friends'). It is, he teaches, an action that reveals who he is and what his love is like. Its loving service is an imperative for healthy life together. It sets an example that can be endlessly improvised upon in each of our lives. It carries the secret of true greatness and of God's blessing. It is not put off or intimidated by whatever threatens, rejects or betrays it. But finally, 'very truly' and above all, it is at the heart of meeting God. *And meeting God cannot be separated from how we relate to one another.*

A while ago, I witnessed a fascinating, moving discussion of this final verse. It happened among a group of around a dozen young Christians from different churches around the world. They had spent a year living together as a Christian community centred on prayer and worship, learning and study, and various forms of service.[2] Their year was about to end, and they were exploring what had happened to them during the year and how they might continue their relationships with one another in the future. This verse had gripped them. As they drew on it to make sense of their experience together and think about their future, its meaning felt both rich and overwhelming.

'Whoever receives one whom I send receives me.' How do we identify who Jesus is sending us and asking us to welcome? Can we exclude anyone we meet? It is dangerous to rule out anyone who enters our lives. Yet in each of our lives, there are people who seem to be especially 'given' to us – family, friends, neighbours, colleagues and, perhaps above all, those in need of our love and service. This group were very clear that they had been invited to receive one another by joining their community for a year. That led at once to the momentous insight: *in receiving one another, they were receiving Jesus.*

They had had many ups and downs during the year, and the basic truth of the foot-washing had become clear to them. As they rubbed up against one another and shared in cooking, cleaning and all the practicalities of living together, they had learned that mutual service, motivated by love for God and one another, was the right thing to aim at. Not only that, but it was the way to receive Jesus and to experience who he is by following his example of receiving others in loving service. That led into a further momentous insight: *in receiving Jesus, they were receiving his Father: 'whoever receives me receives him who sent me'.*

How do we begin to take this in? It involves rereading the Gospel from the beginning. There in the Prologue, the first use of 'receive' is about receiving Jesus through believing, trusting and having faith in him: 'But to all who received him, who believed, trusted and had faith in his name, he gave power to become children of God, who were born … of God' (1:12–13). Then, at the end of the Prologue, we find Jesus at one with his Father in love, 'close to the Father's heart' (1:18). Receiving one is receiving both together, since they are utterly at one with each other.

Taking in the reality of all this receiving – of each other, of Jesus, of his Father – means going beyond the foot-washing in John 13. It also means (as we will explore mainly in part 3 of this book) receiving the rest of the Farewell Discourses: on love and friendship; on receiving the Holy Spirit; on being led into more and more truth; on being sent as Jesus was sent; and on prayer, especially the prayer of Jesus in John 17.

The Farewell Discourses have opened with the love of Jesus demonstrated in humbly washing feet. His teaching about that climaxes in the astonishing revelation of what happens when we follow this example of mutual loving service together: we receive each other, Jesus and his Father into our lives. The Farewell Discourses end in John 17 with an even more astonishing revelation of the fuller reality of this way of love: the sharing with us of the glory and love Jesus shares with his Father. In this prayer, we are drawn into the ultimate dynamics of receiving and mutuality through the desire of Jesus that we be utterly united in trust and love with himself and his Father, and with one another, for the sake of the world God loves. The culminating desire and promise of Jesus is 'I made your name known to them, and I will make it known, so that the love with which you have loved me may be in them, and I in them' (17:26). That happening in us of the knowledge and love of God and the indwelling presence of Jesus is what is at stake in what happens to and through Jesus himself in the rest of the 'hour'.

Interlude: Why no mention of the Eucharist in John's account of the Last Supper?

The Gospels of Matthew, Mark and Luke and Paul's first Letter to the Corinthians all have accounts of the Last Supper Jesus had with his disciples on the night before he died, in which they give accounts (with some variation in details) of what is often called the institution of the Eucharist (also called the Lord's Supper, Holy Communion or the Mass). For many of the world's Christians, this is the central act of regular worship together. There has been a great deal of debate among scholars and others about why John's Gospel does not mention this, with many suggested answers. What follows are my own thoughts in brief.[3]

I agree with those scholars who think that John's Gospel was written with knowledge of other Gospels (he says twice that he knew many other testimonies to Jesus, see 20:30; 21:25) and fully aware of Jesus instituting the Eucharist during his last meal. I would go even further and read John as expecting his readers to know other accounts, so that he does not have to retell everything. As we have already discussed, he wants to give the essentials for coming to faith in Jesus and then maturing in that relationship and having 'life in his name' (20:31). His strategy is to tell far fewer stories but to go deeper into the meaning and implications of those he does. This means that John does not give accounts of many events described in the other Gospels, such as birth stories, temptations, the transfiguration, prayer in Gethsemane and ascension, yet he often gives their meaning. He does this with the Eucharist in John 6, where he goes deeper into its meaning than the other Gospels or Paul, using eucharistic language of thanks (Greek *eucharistein*), bread, sharing, eating and drinking, blood, for your sakes, betrayal, death and eternal life.

What is the effect of John's approach? Two things stand out.

First, by focusing on the foot-washing John encourages those who celebrate the Eucharist to reflect seriously on how it relates to the foot-washing. How does the worship and ritual relate to practical, loving service? And how does a community that is formed around the Eucharist make sure that its forms of power and authority ring true with the humble service of foot-washing? John is in line with many of the prophets of Israel who powerfully attack worship and other religious practices that are not accompanied by right living, justice and compassion. Many churches wisely combine foot-washing with celebration of Holy Communion on Maundy Thursday.

Second, and above all, John reaches through both the Eucharist and foot-washing to emphasise what he sees as most essential of all: who Jesus is and our relationship of trusting him, following him and mutual indwelling with him. In John 6, we hear Jesus say, 'This is the work of God, that you believe and trust in him whom he has sent' (6:29); 'I am the bread of life' (6:35); and 'Those who eat my flesh and drink my blood abide in me, and I in them' (6:56). Then, in his Farewell Discourses, each of those key truths is deepened and intensified, beginning with the foot-washing and culminating in the prayer of Jesus.

The Beloved Disciple, Judas and Peter: Love received and returned, betrayed and denied[4]

It is one thing to teach and do signs among friends over supper, pointing to love at the heart of reality. But we watch the news today, and it is very hard to believe that love is the core truth of our world. Friendships and all other good relationships can go terribly wrong. Suffering, sin, enmity, evil and death are in the headlines. It is in engaging with these realities that love rings true – or not.

Immediately after washing the disciples' feet and teaching about it, Jesus drops a bombshell: 'After saying this Jesus was troubled in spirit, and declared, "Very truly, I tell you, one of you will betray me"' (13:21). The disciples are puzzled and disturbed, and this is the cue for the entry into the story of 'one of his disciples – the one whom Jesus loved' (13:23), the Beloved Disciple. He is described twice as 'reclining next to' Jesus (13:23, 25), literally 'on the bosom' or 'on the breast' of Jesus, echoing 1:18 where Jesus is in the bosom of the Father. It is a picture of love that is utterly mutual, love received and returned. Peter asks the Beloved Disciple to ask Jesus who is meant, and Jesus indicates Judas by dipping a piece of bread and giving it to him. 'After he received the piece of bread, Satan entered into him. Jesus said to him, "Do quickly what you are going to do." … So, after receiving the piece of bread, he immediately went out. And it was night' (13:27–30).

This is a drama of mutual love and the betrayal of love, and by the end of the chapter, a further dimension has been added: the denial and failure of love under pressure. Jesus has followed up his teaching about foot-washing by giving his new commandment to love as he has loved. Peter has enthusiastically responded by promising to lay down his life for Jesus, to which Jesus replies, 'Will you lay down your life for me? Very truly, I tell you, before the cock crows, you will have denied me three times' (13:38).

What is happening? The Beloved Disciple, Judas and Peter are key actors in the intimate, interpersonal drama happening between Jesus and his closest followers in private at this stage of the 'hour'. Here, sin and evil are seen in the betrayal and denial of trust and love. These disciples will continue to play parts in the next stage of the 'hour' – the public drama of the arrest, trial and crucifixion of Jesus the following day. In that stage, sin and evil are seen in how systemic forces – political, military, religious – can be corrupted, resulting in falsehood, enmity, injustice, violence and death. But, as we will see, there is also love at the crucifixion, centred on Jesus, his mother and the Beloved Disciple.

One way of describing what is happening is as a profound, multifaceted confrontation between Jesus – who has earlier been identified with trust, life, healing, light, righteousness, just judgement, truth, joy, peace, power used in service, friendship and, above all, love – and, on the other side, the personal and more-than-personal forces (the latter represented by Satan) identified with fear, death, torture and suffering, darkness, sin and evil, injustice, falsehood, misery, violence, power used in ruthless domination, enmity and, above all, the betrayal, rejection or denial of love.

There is a threefold realism running through the whole drama of John's Gospel that comes to its climactic intensity in this 'hour'.

First, there is realism about individual sin and the evil it can do, especially when it adds its energies to more systemic, institutionalised forces, as with Judas helping the Jewish and Roman authorities. Throughout the Gospel of John (and also the accounts in the other Gospels) there is never any attempt to remove responsibility from

Judas for his betrayal of Jesus or to make excuses for him. It is possible to read phrases such as 'Satan entered into him' (13:27) or 'The devil had already put it into the heart of Judas son of Simon Iscariot to betray him' (13:2) as a sort of determinism, relieving Judas of responsibility for his actions as if he had no choice, but there is no hint of that in the text. The realism of personal freedom and responsibility persists, and it is vital for this Gospel's repeated insistence on the importance of personal response to Jesus.

Second, there is a realism about those more systemic forces that reach beyond individuals and help to shape their thoughts and actions for better or for worse. We are all formed by things about which we may have little choice, such as family, ability or disability, culture, race, nationality, institutions and organisations, gender, education, wealth, religion and experiences or events beyond our control. When any of these are for worse, especially when they can be called 'evil', they can be personified as 'Satan' or 'the devil' (8:44, where he is identified with murder and lies), or the 'ruler of this world' (12:31; 14:30; 16:11), but there is no independent interest in this figure. He is a personification of evil, enabling clear recognition of evil beyond individual responsibility, and John has one overwhelming concern: to affirm that he has been defeated and does not have the last word (12:31; 14:30; 16:11, 33).

This leads to the third, embracing realism: that of Jesus. He suffers the full impact not only of the betrayal of Judas and the denial of Peter but also of an alliance of the most powerful military, political and religious forces in his time and place. The result is his death by crucifixion. We will go further into the meaning of this in the next chapter on Good Friday. But, for those who have paid attention to John's Gospel up to and including the foot-washing, it should be no surprise that the meaning is to do with who Jesus is and the love he embodies. The key to answering the question, 'What is happening?' will be to answer the question, 'Who is happening?'

We might watch the news now and find it hard to believe that our world was created in love for love. But the 'hour' John is describing is also news in the making – good news that is utterly realistic about all the bad news but does not let the bad news be the last word.

Questions for individual reflection and group discussion

Suggested by Revd Canon Amiel Osmaston.

1 Can you remember an occasion when someone showed love, care and honour to you by a humble practical action (like Jesus' foot-washing)? What effect did it have on you?

2 Jesus said, 'Whoever receives one whom I send receives me' (John 13:20). David Ford writes, 'How do we identify who Jesus is sending us and asking us to welcome? … In each of our lives, there are people who seem to be especially "given" to us – family, friends, neighbours, colleagues and, perhaps above all, those in need of our love and service.' Write down the names of those who you believe have been especially 'given' to you. Thank God for each of them and ask God to show you how you can 'receive' and bless them.

3 Is there anything which you feel might be blocking you from fully 'receiving' Jesus and his love? If so, identify and 'name' the blockage and ask God, in the name of Jesus and the power of his Spirit, to remove it.

4 Do you agree with David Ford's words, 'We may watch the news now and find it hard to believe that our world was created in love for love. But the "hour" John is describing is also news in the making – good news that is utterly realistic about all the bad news but does not let the bad news be the last word'? How can we listen to and respond to news and events in ways that affirm the transforming power of love?

7

Friday: Jesus dies

The crucifixion of Jesus happens on Good Friday. That combination of 'crucifixion', a horrific form of torture and execution, with 'Good' points to the profound problem. How can a crucifixion be good news? What was happening on that cross?

These are questions that rightly lead in many directions, and they have been answered in various ways down the centuries. They open up the most difficult questions about suffering, humiliation, sin, evil, enmity, violence and death. All those happened to Jesus and are still happening around the world today – which is bad news. But the New Testament is very clear about why something good was also happening on that cross. It was because of who was on it. So the crucial questions become, 'Who was at the heart of this happening?' and, 'Why is this good news?'

This chapter engages with those questions through a fairly long introduction (which reflects on how John approaches it) followed by three meditations and a brief conclusion.

Good Friday is marked in many different ways by Christians, and I hope that this book can have something to say to everyone who wants to learn from the Gospel of John. For those who have been taking part in a Lent group, by Good Friday the group has usually had its last meeting. Good Friday is not so much about conversation and discussion but more about listening, meditating, praying and silence in the face of Jesus Christ crucified. This rather longer chapter is written to feed that approach, and I have tried to bear in mind both ordinary readers who want to go deeper into the meaning of the crucifixion and those who are responsible for trying to guide others.

The suggested preparation for what follows is to read and reread John 18 and 19 slowly.

Introduction: Who Jesus is and what happens through him

All through its first seventeen chapters, the Gospel of John has been especially concerned with who Jesus is and what happens through him.

- *The Prologue*, as chapter 1 in this book discusses, gives the main headlines.
- *Who is Jesus?* Jesus is the Word of God, God's full self-expression and self-giving. He is God's Son, at one with his Father in love: 'God the only Son, who is close to the Father's heart' (1:18). At the same time, Jesus is utterly human, at one with us: 'And the Word became [Greek *egeneto*] flesh and lived among us, and we have seen his glory' (1:14). God is free to express who God is as a human being, and the good news is that this has actually happened in Jesus Christ.
- *What happens through Jesus?* All creation happens through him;[1] 'life' and 'light for all people' (1:4, 9); 'power to become children of God' (1:12); 'grace and truth' (1:14, 17); and knowledge of God (1:18).

The rest of John 1 and the chapters that follow continue to illuminate who Jesus is and to testify to what is happening through him. *Of special interest in relation to Good Friday are those moments when who Jesus is is connected to what will happen through his crucifixion.*

The first such moment is the dramatic first encounter between John the Baptist and Jesus: 'The next day he saw Jesus coming towards him and declared, "Here is the Lamb of God who takes away the sin of the world!"' (1:29). Later, Jesus dies at the time when the Passover lambs are being killed, recalling the foundational salvation event in Israel's history: the Exodus from Egypt (see Exodus 12). And to be identified as 'the Lamb of God' has many other associations, such as the sacrifice of Isaac (see Genesis 22:8) and the Suffering Servant in Isaiah (see Isaiah 52:13 – 53:12, especially 53:7).[2]

Another moment happens in the next chapter, this time combining the death and resurrection of Jesus. Jesus declares, 'Destroy this temple, and in three days I will raise it up' (2:19), and John explains, 'He was speaking of the temple of his body. After he was raised from the dead, his disciples remembered that he had said this, and they believed the scripture and the word that Jesus had spoken' (2:21–22).

In the profound exchange with Nicodemus in the following chapter, the image of the crucifixion as Jesus being 'lifted up' leads into a key summary of the whole Gospel, with Jesus as both 'Son of Man' and God's 'only Son', and with the love of God at the root of everything that happens through Jesus and especially his death:

And just as Moses lifted up the serpent in the wilderness, so must the Son of Man be lifted up, that whoever believes [and trusts] in him may have eternal life. For God so loved the world that he gave his only Son, so that everyone who believes [and trusts] in him may not perish but may have eternal life. (John 3:14–16)[3]

Then, in the teaching after he feeds the five thousand, Jesus says, 'I am the bread of life' (6:35), but he makes it clear that he is this only through giving his own life: 'I am the living bread that came down from heaven. Whoever eats of this bread will live for ever; and the bread that I will give for the life of the world is my flesh' (6:51).

Again, when Jesus identifies himself as 'the good shepherd', who 'calls his own sheep by name' (10:3) and gives them abundant life, his death is at the heart of this identity-defining and life-giving mission, emphasised again and again: 'I am the good shepherd. The good shepherd lays down his life for the sheep … I lay down my life for the sheep … For this reason the Father loves me, because I lay down my life in order to take it up again' (10:11, 15, 17).

Then comes the announcement by Jesus – 'The hour has come for the Son of Man to be glorified' (12:23) – and his threefold sounding of the depths of his coming death, as explored above in chapter 5 of this book. Again, who he is, as mortal Son of Man and at the same time Son of his Father sharing his eternal glory, is inseparable from his death. And this one death has the potential to be deeply and widely attractive: '"And I, when I am lifted up from the earth, will draw all people to myself." He said this to indicate the kind of death he was to die' (12:32–33).

Even before we arrive in John 13 – 17 at the extended, in-depth preparation for the death of Jesus in his Farewell Discourses during the Last Supper on the night before his crucifixion, John has made it absolutely clear that who Jesus is needs to be utterly central to any understanding of what happens in his crucifixion. His death is to be a singularity, something unique and one-off, a once-and-for-all happening with unlimited attractiveness and impact, and who he uniquely is, at one with God in love and at one with us human beings in love, is at the heart of this reality.

What happens during that intimate meal above all intensifies the emphasis on his death as an act of love. The headline 'Having loved his own who were in the world, he loved them to the end' (13:1) is followed by the dramas of foot-washing and of the betrayal of love by Judas.[4] These lead into the new commandment to love as Jesus has loved (13:34) and then on to the heart of that loving: 'No one has greater love than this, to lay down one's life for one's friends' (15:13).

The Farewell Discourses identify Jesus not only with love but also with truth. This has already been a theme in the first twelve chapters, often through the image of light. It is introduced in the Prologue: 'What has come into being in him was life, and the life was the light of all people' (1:3–4). This is immediately followed by the confrontation of light with everything that opposes it: 'The light shines in the darkness, and the darkness did not overcome it' (1:5). The suffering, sin, enmity, evil and death that Jesus is to face are foreshadowed. In what follows, Jesus is repeatedly identified with the light, most straightforwardly in his announcement, 'I am the light of the world' (8:12) and in his teaching about his crucifixion in John 12:27–36. Then, during the Last Supper as Jesus prepares his disciples for his death, there is a massive emphasis on himself and truth.

This is most straightforward in 14:6: 'Jesus said to him, "I am the way, and the truth, and the life."' Jesus also says, 'You call me Teacher and Lord – and you are right, for that is what I am' (13:13). He says that his disciples are his friends with whom he has shared the truth he knows: 'I have made known to you everything I have heard from my father' (15:15), and he promises them the gift of the Holy Spirit, 'the Spirit of truth' who 'will guide you into all the truth … He will glorify me' (16:13–14).

Then, in the prayer of Jesus in John 17, the depth and intensity of both love and truth come together with who Jesus is as he heads for his death. This is the intimate heart of meeting God in John, and we have already begun to open up its astonishing meaning in previous chapters and to enter into it through praying the Lord's Prayer in its light. There is always more to be discovered. In relation to what is about to happen on Good Friday, the prayer faces into the darkness: the betrayal by Judas, the hatred of 'the world' and the enmity of 'the evil one'. Faced with this, Jesus focuses on truth and love.

The truth is based on knowing who God is, who Jesus is and how they are related. The life Jesus gives is 'eternal life, that they may know you, the only true God, and Jesus Christ, whom you have sent' (17:3). The truth has been given in 'your word', so that 'now they know that everything you have given me is from you … and know in truth that I came from you; and they have believed that you sent me' (17:7–8). The focus on truth reaches its greatest intensity after Jesus prays for his disciples to be protected from the hatred of 'the world' and from 'the evil one':

> They do not belong to the world, just as I do not belong to the world. Sanctify them in the truth; your word is truth. As you have sent me into the world, so I have sent them into the world. And for their sakes I sanctify myself, so that they also may be sanctified in truth.
> (John 17:16–19)

We will see how the identification of Jesus with the truth happens in his trial and crucifixion.

The love then comes in the final extraordinary verses, 17:20–26. Here, the prayer opens out to embrace everyone who comes to believe, trust and have faith in Jesus through the 'word' of the disciples (which, of course, includes this prayer and the whole Gospel of John). Jesus desires us all to be one with himself and his Father, and with one another, for the sake of the world God loves. The love comes in three waves:

1 We are loved with the same love with which the Father loves Jesus: 'you … have loved them even as you have loved me' (17:23).
2 This love goes to the heart of all reality, and it is nothing less than the love with which 'you loved me before the foundation of the world' (17:24).
3 The purpose of all this is full participation in knowing the truth of who God is and in sharing the love of God embodied in Jesus himself: 'I made your name known to them, and I will make it known, so that the love with which you have loved me may be in them, and I in them' (17:26).

The ultimate truth is God and God's love given to us through Jesus in person. *We will see how the identification of Jesus with love happens in his crucifixion.*

Here, the preparation for Good Friday is complete in the fullest possible unity between truth, love and who Jesus is.[5] We readers of John have been given language, concepts, images, teachings, signs and foretastes to prepare us to take in who Jesus is and what is happening through him. But while Jesus has done signs of the unity, taught the unity and finally prayed for the unity, it has not yet happened fully in time. The 'hour' is not yet finished. The stage has been set for what happens on Good Friday.

1 Meditation on the arrest and trial: Truth in person

We have been following the way John opens up, right from the start of the Gospel, who Jesus is and the meaning of his death, culminating in the final teaching and prayer of Jesus. There are numerous worthwhile ways of meditating on what follows in John 18 and 19. Ours will focus on the three interwoven themes we have found in the first seventeen chapters: who Jesus is, truth and love.

The suggestion in this first meditation on the arrest and trial of Jesus is to read 18:1 – 19:16 slowly, twice.

1 a) Who Jesus is

The first time you read the passage, notice and meditate on the way we are led to focus on who Jesus is.

In the arrest (18:1–12):

> Jesus 'asked them, "For whom are you looking?" They answered, "Jesus of Nazareth." Jesus replied, "I am he" [Greek *egō eimi*, meaning "I am"] … When Jesus said to them, "I am he" [*egō eimi*], they stepped back and fell to the ground … Again he asked them, "For whom are you looking?" And they said, "Jesus of Nazareth." Jesus answered, "I told you that I am he [*egō eimi*]."'
> (John 18:4–8)

The triple 'I am' could not be a clearer headline for what follows. Who Jesus is is central. This is then reinforced by Jesus testifying to his own most essential relationship: 'Am I not to drink the cup that the Father has given me?' (18:11).

In the trial (18:1 – 19:16):

> Caiaphas was the one who had advised the Jews that it was better to have one person die for the people.
> (John 18:14)

John has earlier (11:47–52) reflected on the irony of Caiaphas unintentionally testifying to the importance of Jesus by speaking the prophetic truth about his unique death 'not for the nation only, but to gather into one the dispersed children of God.' There is a stark contrast between the triple 'I am' of Jesus and the three denials of Simon Peter: '"I am not" … He denied it and said, "I am not" … Again Peter denied it, and at that moment the cock crowed' (18:17, 25–27).

> Then Pilate entered the headquarters again, summoned Jesus, and asked him, 'Are you the King of the Jews?'
> (John 18:33)

Pilate also issues a denial: 'I am not a Jew, am I?' (18:35).

When Jesus speaks of the origins of his kingdom being 'not from this world … not from here' (18:36), and 'Pilate asks him, 'So you are a king?' (18:37), Jesus responds by identifying himself with 'the truth' (see the next meditation). Then, when Pilate finds 'no case against him' and offers 'to release for you the King of the Jews' (18:38–39), the response of his accusers is another denial: 'They shouted in reply, "Not this man, but Barabbas!"' (18:40).

The focus on who Jesus is is sustained through John 19:

- When Jesus is flogged, he is given the markers of royal identity (a crown of thorns, royal purple) and mocked by the soldiers, 'Hail, King of the Jews!' (19:3).
- When Pilate brings out Jesus 'wearing the crown of thorns and the purple robe', he introduces him, 'Here is the man!' (19:5).
- The cry of the chief priests and the police, 'Crucify him! Crucify him!' (19:6) is justified by who Jesus claims to be: 'We have a law, and according to that law he ought to die because he has claimed to be the Son of God' (19:7).

Pilate's next question to Jesus is, 'Where are you from?' (19:9). Jesus does not answer, but we readers know the answer, and we know that Pilate's question should be '*Who* are you from?' Jesus is, as John's Gospel repeats numerous times, sent by his Father. Just as earlier he had said that his kingdom was 'not from this world' (18:36), here he points to the ultimate power of God: 'You would have no power over me unless it had been given you from above' (19:11). The response of the accusers is then to set up the ultimate power contrast between Jesus and the Roman emperor: 'Everyone who claims to be a king sets himself against the emperor' (19:12).

For Pilate, that is the decisive argument. Put like that, he must choose the emperor, even while still affirming Jesus as King of the Jews – 'Here is your King … Shall I crucify your King?' (19:14–15). And the Jewish accusers also make a decisive declaration of allegiance and identity: 'We have no king but the emperor' (19:15). The implication is the emperor, not even God.[6]

John has made very clear, in the arrest and all through the trial, that the utterly decisive reality is who Jesus is, and that is profoundly different from who Peter, Pilate, Barabbas, the chief priests, the police and even the Roman emperor are.

1 b) Truth

The second time, rereading 18:1 to 19:16, notice and meditate on the way we are led to focus on truth in relation to Jesus.

In the arrest:

- *'After Jesus had spoken these words'* (18:1). That carries into the drama that follows the memory of everything that Jesus has taught and prayed in the Farewell Discourses.
- *'Then Jesus, knowing all that was to happen to him, came forward'* (18:4). All the Gospels see Jesus entering into his passion and death with full awareness of the reality he is facing. We will explore in the third meditation below how what 'was to happen to him' relates to who he is.
- *'This was to fulfil the word that he had spoken, "I did not lose a single one of those whom you gave me"'* (18:9). We recall Jesus praying in the previous chapter, 'Your word is truth' (17:17). Throughout the New Testament, the life, death and resurrection of Jesus are understood as fulfilling the Scriptures.

In the trial:

- The reference to Caiaphas's advice (18:14) directs readers back to the earlier affirmation that what Caiaphas said was true in ways he himself did not recognise: 'He did not say this on his own, but being high priest that year he prophesied that Jesus was about to die for the nation, and not for the nation only, but to gather into one the dispersed children of God' (11:51–52).
- Jesus is first interrogated 'about his disciples and about his teaching' and affirms that he has always 'spoken openly to the world' (18:19–20). The main concern of his accusers is his teaching

about who he is. And, in his exchange with Pilate about whether he is a king, the key move Jesus makes is to describe his kingship as being about truth: 'For this I was born, and for this I came into the world, to testify to the truth. Everyone who belongs to the truth listens to my voice' (18:37).

Who Jesus is and what the truth is could hardly be more closely identified, recalling his earlier teaching, 'I am … the truth' (14:6). For readers, there is deep, unconscious irony in Pilate's question, 'What is truth?' The question should be, '*Who* is the truth?'

As we have seen, the same switch to 'who' applies to Pilate's later question, 'Where are you from?' (19:9). The 'who' answer to that is 'the Father', which in turn connects with a further irony: the truest identification of Jesus is when his accusers quote his claim 'to be the Son of God' (19:7).

It is striking that in the intimate setting of the Last Supper, the primary emphasis was on love. But here in the public sphere, when Jesus confronts those with political, military and religious authority and power, the primary emphasis is on truth. Power is not denied, but it is seen as originating in God. In the kingship of God's Son, Jesus, truth is inseparable from power and authority. The importance of this has probably never been greater in our world of public education, artificial intelligence, mass media, social media, algorithms devised to make most profit, fake news and, above all, the convergence of wealth, power and the control of information and knowledge. And, as the Farewell Discourses have shown, truth is also essential to love.

So, what is happening in this trial? False accusation, a corrupt alliance between powerful forces, painful flogging, public humiliation and unjust condemnation are all happening to Jesus. But he, Jesus, Son of Man and Son of God, is also happening to all of them. What will the outcome be?

The first, most obvious, outcome is this: Pilate 'handed him over to them to be crucified' (19:16).

2 Meditation on the crucifixion: Love on the cross

The suggestion in this second meditation is to read 19:16–42 slowly twice.

2 a) Who Jesus is

The first time, notice and meditate on the way we are led to focus on Jesus and who he is:

> There they crucified him, and with him two others, one on either side, with Jesus between them.
> (John 19:18)

The Greek says, *meson de ton Iēsoun*, meaning 'Jesus central, or in the middle'. Crucifixion was happening to all three, but the crucial, transformative happening was centred in the named person in the middle.

> Pilate also had an inscription written and put on the cross. It read, 'Jesus of Nazareth, the King of the Jews.'
> (John 19:19)

A great deal is made of this inscription, written in Hebrew, Latin and Greek, and read by 'many of the Jews' (19:20). 'King of the Jews' is repeated three times. It is disputed by the chief priests, but Pilate insists on it: 'What I have written I have written' (19:22).

Even what happens to the clothes of Jesus, and especially his seamless tunic, is significant. It is understood as fulfilling a scripture about 'my clothes … my clothing' (19:24).

Next comes the event I am calling 'love on the cross' in which the focus is on who Jesus is in relation to his mother and the Beloved Disciple (see the next chapter), and then come the last words and death of Jesus (see the next meditation).

Even after his death, there is a fascinating, mysterious focus on what happens to and through his dead body, with scriptures underlining the importance of what is occurring and to whom (see the next meditation). The last Greek word in the account of the burial is 'Jesus'.

2 b) Love

The second time, rereading, notice and meditate on how we are led to focus on love in relation to Jesus.

This comes especially in a scene unique to John, when Jesus speaks from the cross to his mother and to his Beloved Disciple:

> Meanwhile, standing near the cross of Jesus were his mother, and his mother's sister, Mary the wife of Clopas, and Mary Magdalene. When Jesus saw his mother and the disciple whom he loved standing beside her, he said to his mother, 'Woman, here is your son.' Then he said to the disciple, 'Here is your mother.' And from that hour the disciple took her into his own home.
> (John 19:25–27)

What does this say about love?

The headline of the Farewell Discourses says, 'Jesus knew that his hour had come to depart from this world and go to the Father. Having loved his own who were in the world, he loved them to the end' (13:1). Now the end has come very near, and it is hard to think of any who are more 'his own' than his mother and the disciple he loved. That these two are the supreme examples of those he loves shows that the love Jesus desires above all is *love that is utterly mutual*. It is to be like a good mother-child relationship or a good friend-to-friend relationship.

It is utterly mutual between each of them and Jesus, mother-son and friend-friend. Jesus had called his disciples friends when he said,

'No one has greater love than this, to lay down one's life for one's friends' (15:13). And this disciple's whole identity in this Gospel is defined by being loved and loving.

But it is also utterly mutual between his mother and his friend. This is the creation of a new sort of family. It has kinship and friendship. It crosses generations. It has male and female. Above all, its source is Jesus, and the bond between his mother and his friend is rooted in their relationship of love with him. Jesus creates new relationships, a new community embracing family and more than family. And he does this from the cross. Jesus Christ crucified is at the heart of this new family. He is the inspiration and the measure of the mutual love that unites its members.

What are the limits of this love? Are there any? Jesus had said about his crucifixion, 'And I, when I am lifted up from the earth, will draw all people to myself' (12:32). Now, Jesus is lifted up on the cross, and these, in the Gospel of John, are the first words he speaks from there. He is drawing to himself his mother and his Beloved Disciple in a new way by uniting them together in a new way. This is not to stop with them. This love is for all. It can of course be rejected, but at its heart is an unlimited desire for fully mutual love. And the sign of Jesus opening his arms to all is him nailed to the cross, in utter solidarity, entering into the depths of suffering, humiliation, darkness and death.

What are the depths of this love? *Nothing less than the depths of the love of God who is love!* The crowning statement of Jesus, in his teaching about the meaning of him washing the feet of his disciples in love, was 'Very truly, I tell you, whoever receives one I send receives me; and whoever receives me receives him who sends me' (13:20). Now, we read, 'And from that hour the disciple took her into his own home' (19:27). In Greek, the verb for 'receives' in 13:20 is the same as the verb 'took' in 19:27 – both are forms of *lambanein*. So we can translate, 'And from that hour the disciple received her into his own home.' What is happening now, in this most important 'hour', is Jesus sending his mother and his Beloved Disciple to each other. In receiving each other, this new household is also receiving not only Jesus but also, at one with Jesus, the Father who sends him.

That is a sign of the fulfilment of the culminating desire of Jesus in his prayer to his Father in John 17 as he heads for his crucifixion: 'that they may be one, as we are one, I in them and you in me, that they may become completely one, so that the world may know that you have sent me and have loved them even as you have loved me' (17:22–23). The future horizon of this 'hour' is that utter unity in a love without limits, the love with which, says Jesus to his Father, 'you loved me before the foundation of the world' (17:24).

But the 'hour' is still not finished.

3 Meditation on the death of Jesus: What was happening?

After this, when Jesus knew that all was now finished, he said (in order to fulfil the scripture), 'I am thirsty.' A jar full of sour wine was standing there. So they put a sponge full of the wine on a branch of hyssop and held it to his mouth. When Jesus had received the wine, he said, 'It is finished.' Then he bowed his head and gave up his spirit.

(John 19:28–30)

What was happening on the cross? In this short passage, we see Jesus suffering thirst and then dying. The real suffering and death of Jesus is testified to in all the Gospels and throughout the rest of the New Testament, and his dead body is the focus in the rest of John 19.

But, in the light of John's way of preparing readers to understand this event, always uniting the death of Jesus with pointers to who he is, the question that leads to the heart of what is happening is, '*Who* was happening on the cross?' The lesson of every chapter of the

Gospel of John is this: *Jesus Christ, utterly one with God and utterly one with us, is who was happening on the cross.* Only this can reach into the depth and breadth of the uniqueness and embracing importance of this event.

Thirst and death happened to him – and more: betrayal and denial of trust and love, enmity and hatred, torture, injustice, humiliation, and more of sin, darkness and evil, both individual and systemic. *But Jesus was also happening to suffering, sin, evil, death and the rest.*

Here, in this passage, the relationship with God is suggested by saying, 'Jesus knew that all was now finished' (19:28), and that what he said was a fulfilment of the Scriptures. His relationship with us is there in his cry and then, decisively, in his death. He was mortal and died. We are mortal and die.

As we hear Jesus cry 'I am thirsty', we think back to him in conversation with the Samaritan woman at Jacob's well:

> Jesus said to her, 'Everyone who drinks of this water will be thirsty again, but those who drink of the water that I will give them will never be thirsty. The water that I will give will become in them a spring of water gushing up to eternal life.'
> (John 4:13–14)

Jesus is both thirsty and a thirst-quencher. He wants a drink, and he wants to give the water of eternal life. He turns water into the best wine, and he himself drinks vinegar. He calls Lazarus out of the tomb, and he goes the way of the cross to his tomb. At his arrest, he says, 'Am I not to drink the cup that the Father has given me?' (18:11).

An extraordinary poem goes to the heart of this who-centred happening. Around six hundred years ago, Julian of Norwich, steeped in the Gospel of John, wrote down her *Revelations of Divine Love*, a love-centred account of her experiences based on the suffering and death of Jesus. In the twentieth century, Denise Levertov, steeped in both the Gospel of John and Julian's *Revelations of Divine Love*, wrote her poem 'On a Theme from Julian's Chapter XX'.[7] Levertov asks about the uniqueness of the suffering of Jesus. Why, among all the suffering, torture, evil and death in human history, is he alone 'King of Grief'? Her answer centres on who Jesus is, expanding on two core phrases from Julian:

1 First: His '*oneing with the Godhead*', his utter unity with God:
2 This, writes Levertov, 'opened Him utterly' to all the suffering and death brought about by sin and evil throughout history, past, present and future.
3 Second: His unity and solidarity with us human beings.
4 *Every sorrow and desolation*
5 *He saw, and sorrowed in kinship.*

As Julian and Levertov both perceive, who Jesus uniquely is does not lessen his suffering but intensifies it, allowing him to take on more in love. 'When Jesus had received the wine, he said, "It is finished"'(19:30). What is finished, completed and fulfilled on the cross is what Jesus prays about in John 17: glorifying his Father 'on earth by finishing the work that you gave me to do' (17:4). This, he says, requires sanctifying 'myself so that they [his disciples] also may be sanctified in truth' (17:19). Above all, it is about their becoming 'completely one'[8] (17:23) in love with him, with his Father and with one another for the sake of the world. *Truth and the ultimate work of love have come together, embodied in this particular person on this cross.*

'Then he bowed his head and gave up his spirit' (19:30). He died.

Conclusion

Our leading questions about the arrest, trial and crucifixion of Jesus have been, 'Who was at the heart of this happening, and why is this good news?' We have begun to answer them, but the 'hour' is still not over.

Good Friday continues with John giving insistent testimony to a soldier piercing Jesus' side, after which 'at once blood and water came out' (19:34). Blood and water are deep symbols in this Gospel and elsewhere in the Scriptures, well worth meditating upon.

This outpouring of blood and water is the last thing that happens while Jesus is 'lifted up' on the cross. The 'lifting up' is an event that, as we have seen, has been given immense importance at key points in earlier chapters. In John 3, it is a sign that summarises the whole Gospel. It is about receiving eternal life through believing and trusting in the Son of Man 'lifted up' and this being due to God giving his only Son in love for the world (3:14–16). In John 8, it is about the 'I am' of Jesus: 'When you have lifted up the Son of Man, then you will realise that I am' (8:28). In John 12, it is about attraction to the crucified Jesus: 'I, when I am lifted up from the earth, will draw all' (12:32).

In the light of all that, the blood and water can now be seen as the sacrificial, life-giving love of God pouring out of the Son of Man, who is also the divine 'I am'. John's insistent address to us readers is, 'He who saw this has testified so that you also may believe [trust and have faith]. His testimony is true, and he knows that he tells the truth' (19:35). It is a *cri de coeur*: '*Trust this truth! Trust this love! Trust Jesus!*'

Then, Jesus is buried in a tomb in a nearby garden. The 'hour' continues.

Questions for individual reflection and group discussion

Suggested by Revd Canon Amiel Osmaston.

1 What does Good Friday and the cross mean to you? This chapter asks, 'Who is Jesus and what happens through him?' Which of David Ford's 'answers' are most significant for you?

2 Do you find it helpful to see the cross as 'an act of love and an assertion of truth'? How does (or how might) this love and truth shape your own relationship with Jesus?

3 The gospel writer John states, 'He who saw this has testified so that you also may believe [trust and have faith]. His testimony is true, and he knows that he tells the truth' (John 19:35). Could you say the same as John? Can you speak truthfully to other people about your experiences of 'God at work' so that they may also believe and trust in Jesus?

4 How can and should Christians act in the light of David's statement about truth: 'In … Jesus, truth is inseparable from power and authority. The importance of this has probably never been greater in our world of public education, artificial intelligence, mass media, social media, algorithms devised to make most profit, fake news and, above all, the convergence of wealth, power and the control of information and knowledge'?

8

Sunday: Jesus alive

> And so, because it was the Jewish day of Preparation, and the tomb was nearby, they laid Jesus there. Early on the first day of the week, while it was still dark, Mary Magdalene came to the tomb and saw that the stone had been removed from the tomb.
> (John 19:42 – 20:1)

What happened between Jesus being laid in the tomb and Mary Magdalene finding the stone removed? The New Testament is clear about two things: the body of Jesus was not in the tomb, and the crucified Jesus was alive in a new way. John's Gospel vividly testifies to both.

First, there is testimony to the absence of the body. Mary Magdalene runs to tell Peter and the Beloved Disciple. They run to the tomb and find the linen grave clothes of Jesus but not his body. Then, there is a series of surprise encounters. Jesus meets with Mary Magdalene; Jesus meets with the disciples without Thomas; and Jesus meets with Thomas in the presence of his fellow disciples.

So, what had happened between Friday and Sunday? Something utterly surprising and unprecedented, certainly. But 'what' and 'something' are inadequate. The whole New Testament, and John with special emphasis, focuses on 'who' and 'someone': Jesus.

Preparing for the great surprise

We have already seen in discussing Good Friday how, from the beginning of the Gospel, John prepares readers for what was to happen on the cross by repeatedly combining looking ahead to the crucifixion of Jesus with major statements about who Jesus is. Above all, these are 'I am' sayings of Jesus. After feeding the five thousand, Jesus says, 'I am the bread of life ... and the bread that I will give for the life of the world is my flesh' (6:35, 51). As his death draws nearer, he says, 'I am the good shepherd. The good shepherd lays down his life for the sheep' (10:11). Then, as we found, the way John tells of the Last Supper, arrest, trial and crucifixion of Jesus intensifies the concentration on who he is. John prepares us readers for the resurrection of Jesus in the same way by focusing on who Jesus is.

In John 2, the emphasis is on his relationship with his Father, as both his death and his resurrection are anticipated (2:13–22). He goes much deeper into this most important, identity-defining relationship in John 5, stressing the love between them, the surprises to come and their unity as life-givers:

> The Father loves the Son and shows him all that he himself is doing; and he will show him greater works than these, so that you will be astonished. Indeed, just as the Father raises the dead and gives them life, so also the Son gives life to whomsoever he wishes ... For just as the Father has life in himself, so he has granted the Son also to have life in himself.
> (John 5:20–26)

Later, in his identity as the 'good shepherd', his union with the Father in love is again central to both his death and his resurrection: 'For this reason the Father loves me, because I lay down my life in order to take it up again' (10:17).

The climactic statement is 'I am the resurrection and the life' (11:25). This comes in the climactic sign of his public ministry, as he prepares to call his friend Lazarus ('he whom you love', 11:3) out of his tomb. *It is an identification of himself with resurrection, life and love in the face of death,* and this is intensified through the Farewell

Discourses, where truth in particular is joined with these: 'I am the way, and the truth, and the life' (14:6).

Jesus happens in a new way

By the time Jesus hangs on the cross, John has made it clear: death is happening to one who is life in person, truth in person, love in person and utterly one with the living God who is light and love.[1] *But this person is also happening to death. And not only to death, but also to darkness, suffering, sin, enmity and evil.* Because of who he is, the result makes deep sense: death cannot hold him, and darkness, suffering, enmity, evil and death do not have the last word. He, in person, is the last word, just as he is the first word (1:1). His resurrection happens.[2]

Jesus happens in a new way. John 20 tells how he happens to Mary Magdalene, to his disciples, and then to Thomas. John 21 shows how he continues to happen. And the author makes clear his own primary purpose: to enable this to continue to happen for readers (20:30–31; 21:24–25).

There is inexhaustible meaning in these final two chapters of John's Gospel. Here, in line with this book's title, we will now concentrate on how John 20 is about God and enables readers to meet God. There will be more to say about John 20 and 21 in the next chapter and conclusion of this book.

'Mary!' – 'Rabbouni!'

The meeting of Mary Magdalene with the resurrected Jesus is probably the most moving moment in John's Gospel. She has seen him die a tortured death. Now, in addition, she thinks that someone has taken his dead body. She is traumatised, bewildered, grief-stricken, weeping. She sees Jesus and thinks that he is the gardener. We have engaged with this meeting before in chapter 1, but it is worth revisiting.

What Jesus says brings us right back to the beginning of the Gospel. There, his first words to his first disciples were, 'What are you looking for?' (1:38). That opened up the key theme of desire, which we explored in chapter 3 of this book. Now, to Mary, Jesus repeats those words, but with a crucial change from 'what' to 'who': 'For whom are you looking?' (20:15). That unites desire with the most important theme of all, which we explored in chapter 2: the 'who' question. Mary has been looking for a dead 'what'; she is surprised and questioned by a living 'who'. And it is not just about who Jesus is but about who 'you' are. Jesus calls each by name, and his next word is 'Mary!' It is a beautiful illustration of the heart of what happens, and continues to happen, through the resurrection of Jesus: *who-to-who meeting with him*. She cries out in recognition, '"Rabbouni!"' (which means Teacher)' (20:16).

He is still her Teacher, as before, but what he goes on to say is something new: 'Do not hold on to me, because I have not yet ascended to the Father. But go to my brothers and say to them, "I am ascending to my Father and your Father, to my God and your God"' (20:17). There are at least two important messages in that.

'Do not hold on to me'

First, this marks a change in how Mary is about to relate to Jesus, a change that will put her in the same position as all followers of Jesus ever since.

Up to now, she has been able to touch him and see him on occasion because he has been present like anyone else, in one place at a time. But Jesus ascending to his Father means that, in the future, he will be present as God is present, free to relate to all people, at all times and in all places. Jesus is preparing her for that. He will be real (indeed, supremely real, divinely real), but not ordinarily to be touched or seen in person here in the world. *This is, in fact, far better.*

At the Last Supper, when he promised to give the Holy Spirit, he said, 'If you loved me you would rejoice that I am going to the Father

… I tell you the truth: it is to your advantage that I go away' (14:28; 16:7). Jesus ascending to the Father means that he will be invisible but free to be present everywhere, as God is present and invisible. How he desires to be present for those who will receive him is taught in the parable of the vine in John 15 and then prayed in John 17: he wants the intimacy of mutual indwelling in trust and love, the deepest imaginable, permanently abiding relationship. *That uninterrupted personal presence – not occasional meetings – is Mary's future, as it is also for anyone else who receives Jesus with trust and love* .

'My Father and your Father … my God and your God'

Second, that relationship – which is nothing less than participating in the divine life, eternal life – is signalled by the message Jesus sends her to deliver.

Up to now in John's Gospel, the Father has only been the Father of Jesus. Now, for the first time, Jesus says, 'My Father and your Father … my God and your God' (20:17). His disciples are to share fully in the relationship of Jesus with his Father, as he prayed in John 17. The ascension of Jesus is not a distancing; it is essential to a new sort of radical divine intimacy, available to all people in all times and places. The deep mutuality of 'Mary!' – 'Rabbouni!' is to be shareable without limit through the creation of a new family of brothers and sisters. This is the best possible news, and Mary becomes its first communicator: 'Mary Magdalene went and announced to the disciples, "I have seen the Lord"; and she told them that he had said these things to her' (20:18).

It is as if the resurrection and ascension of Jesus are further dimensions of him being 'lifted up' that began in his crucifixion, with his ascension being the ultimate uplift. Resurrection and ascension are a further fulfilment of his promise, 'I, when I am lifted up from the earth, will draw all people to myself' (12:32). That began with him on the cross forming a new family household of his mother and his Beloved Disciple (19:25–27), combining kinship and friendship as discussed in the previous chapter of this book. Now, the wider circle of disciples are embraced in this new family headed by 'my Father and your[3] Father'. And the future horizon is nothing less than 'all people'. How that is to happen is signalled by the next meeting with Jesus.

'As the Father has sent me, so I send you'

The appearance of Jesus *eis to meson*, meaning 'into the middle, into the centre' of the gathering of the disciples behind locked doors in John 20:19–23 is a happening in which core essentials of the Gospel of John are concentrated:

- Its centre is Jesus.
- It is another who-to-who meeting with Jesus.
- Twice he says, 'Peace be with you' (20:19, 21).

In his Farewell Discourses at the Last Supper, Jesus had twice promised his disciples peace. First, peace is to accompany the gift of the Holy Spirit, and it is to be a peace identified with himself: 'Peace I leave with you; my peace I give you. I do not give to you as the world gives' (14:27). Second, it is a peace 'in me' that is stronger than anything the world can throw at them: 'I have said this to you, so that in me you may have peace. In the world you face persecution. But take courage; I have conquered the world!' (16:33). Peace (Hebrew *shalom*) in Israel's and Jesus' Scriptures is a comprehensive term for what God both desires and promises, and it is even a name of God. It embraces flourishing relationships with God, with other people and groups, and with creation. In community life, peace includes love, justice and righteousness, reconciliation, health and prosperity. Here, it is used by Jesus as a greeting, perhaps to be understood the first time as being aimed at the fear of the disciples.

'He showed them his hands and his side' (20:20). As we have seen, this Gospel prepares readers for the crucifixion and resurrection of Jesus from the start. Here, in this showing, we see the crucifixion and the resurrection finally and decisively embodied together in the person of Jesus. Jesus – crucified, risen and alive in a new way – is the outcome of Good Friday. *The happening on the cross, and whatever happened between that and Easter Sunday morning, results in the living Jesus.*

'Then the disciples rejoiced when they saw the Lord' (20:20). The resurrection of Jesus is the quintessentially joyful happening. In his Farewell Discourses, Jesus compared it to the joy at new life, the birth of a baby:

> Your pain will turn to joy. When a woman is in labour, she has pain, because her hour has come. But when her child is born, she no longer remembers the anguish because of the joy of having brought a human being into the world. So you have pain now, but I will see you again and your hearts will rejoice, and no one will take your joy from you.
> (John 16:20–22)

There is even a further astonishing promise for the ongoing relationship: 'Very truly, I tell you, if you ask anything of the Father in my name, he will give it to you … Ask and you will receive, so that your joy may be complete' (16:23–24).

Then, in his final prayer, as he anticipates his death and resurrection, Jesus himself asks 'that they may have my joy made complete in themselves' (17:13). That is the mutual, lasting, complete joy that is now beginning in this meeting. It is, says Jesus, 'my joy' – joy in Jesus, the one who has just shown the marks of his torture and crucifixion. *Jesus himself is their joy, so this is a joy inextinguishable by suffering, sin, enmity, evil, or death.*

The second 'Peace be with you' opens the way into Jesus giving these disciples, and disciples after them, their vocation and mission:

'As the Father has sent me, so I send you' (20:21). He has already prayed to his Father, 'As you have sent me into the world, so I have sent them into the world' (17:18). Here is the triple thrust of Christian living:

- Being sent into the world.
- Being together, in community – the 'you' is plural.
- Being sent as the Father sent Jesus.

This is a vocation and mission of life-giving love for the world. We will return to this in the next chapter and in the conclusion of this book – it can be seen as the DNA of the Church. For now, we focus on the astonishing, God-centred 'as … so'.

How can we understand the sending of Jesus by the Father? We need to reflect on the whole Gospel from the beginning because that is the story of this sending. It is about the Holy Spirit resting on Jesus; Jesus gathering a community of learners; Jesus teaching and having conversations and debates; Jesus doing signs of abundant life for all; Jesus washing feet like a slave; Jesus loving his friends; Jesus praying; Jesus testifying to the truth; Jesus suffering and dying; Jesus alive – and there is much, much more. It is possible to go deeper and deeper into each event, each conversation, each meeting, each teaching. We are invited into continual rereading in order to grasp the sending of Jesus. And the depth at the heart of his sending is his relationship with his Father. *We are invited, above all through his prayer in John 17 and now through John 20, into that relationship as our true home, from where we too are sent.* It is not only continual rereading that opens these depths, but also continual prayer and continual living in community with others who read and pray with us.

But that 'as … so' will not let us stop even there. The 'as' means that we are not sent in exactly the same way as Jesus. How could we be? We do not repeat his life in first-century Palestine. We are sent into new times, situations and places, and we are sent with and to new people. Every day is unique, so every single day requires us to discern what that 'as ... so' means for us now. Christian living requires ever-deeper understanding of who Jesus is and how he was sent. But it also requires ever-deeper understanding of our situations, of the world we are in and of how we are being called to improvise continually on how Jesus was sent while remaining true to who he is. We are called to be imaginative and creative, and to be willing to risk being innovative and daring, in the spirit of Jesus who sprang repeated surprises. How to do all that in the twenty-first century will be the concern of the next chapter and the conclusion of this book. But none of it would be possible without what Jesus, according to John 20:22, did and said next.

'When he had said this, he breathed on them and said to them, "Receive the Holy Spirit"' (20:22). Jesus breathed the Holy Spirit into his disciples. It is a momentous event. Just as with the crucifixion and resurrection of Jesus, all through this Gospel, from the very first chapter, this giving of the Holy Spirit has been promised and expected.

John the Baptist announced, as a word from God, 'He on whom you see the Spirit descend and remain is the one who baptises with the Holy Spirit' (1:33). So all through what follows, we are to understand both that Jesus is utterly one with the Holy Spirit and that the time will come when he will share this Spirit. That comes now, and it can be seen as the crowning happening of the 'hour'. *The Father sent Jesus filled with the Holy Spirit. Now the disciples are being sent as Jesus was sent.*

In conversation with Nicodemus, the Spirit had been compared to the wind (the word for spirit in Greek, *pneuma*, also means 'wind' or 'breath'), blowing where it chooses, springing surprises and enabling a completely new beginning, being 'born from above, born again' (3:3, 7; the Greek word *anōthen* can mean both 'from above' and 'again'). Now, in what the resurrected Jesus says to his disciples, the word used for 'breathed' is the same as the word used for God breathing the breath of life into Adam at creation (Genesis 2:7). *For the New Testament, the only happening comparable to the resurrection and the new life given through it is creation by God.*

An important passage later in John 3 says, 'He whom God has sent speaks the words of God, for he gives the Spirit without measure' (John 3:34). The Spirit is the divine superabundance, resonating with the Prologue's headline about Jesus, 'From his fullness we have all received, grace upon grace' (1:16), and with the later dramatic cry of Jesus at the Festival of Booths:

> 'Let anyone who is thirsty come to me, and let the one who believes in me drink. As the scripture has said, "Out of the believer's heart shall flow rivers of living water."' Now he said this about the Spirit, which believers in him were to receive; for as yet there was no Spirit, because Jesus was not yet glorified. (John 7:37–39)

Now, Jesus has been glorified, and this immeasurable superabundance of God's Spirit is shared intimately, face to face, with his disciples.

Most important of all are the Farewell Discourses. They have much to say about the Holy Spirit that is oriented towards the life of the community of disciples in the aftermath of the resurrection, and the final part of this book will explore that ongoing drama. But for now, we are especially focusing on meeting God. Jesus at the Last Supper promises not only meeting God through himself (as he says to Phillip in 14:9, 'Whoever has seen me has seen the Father') but also a new self-giving of God to us in the Holy Spirit, utterly at one with himself and his Father. If we really receive Jesus, we also receive his Father and his Spirit. *This is certainly meeting God, but if it is really God we are meeting, then there is no end to the meeting.* It becomes a permanent relationship, an abiding, a mutual indwelling in love, a life and love beginning now and lasting for ever – our true home.

The promise is clear: 'I will ask the Father, and he will give you another Advocate [Greek *paraklētos*, also meaning 'Helper', 'Encourager' or 'Comforter'], to be with you for ever … You know him, because he abides with you and will be in you' (14:16–17). This is living in mutual love, and involves the Holy Spirit with the Father and Jesus: 'Those who love me will keep my word, and my Father will love them, and we will come to them and make our home[4] with them' (14:23). Just as God is free to express who God is in Jesus Christ, giving God's self to come among us as a human being, so God, who 'is Spirit' (4:24) is free to share God's being and life through Jesus breathing the Holy Spirit into us. *We, astonishingly, are to share the home life, the family life, of God.*

The fulfilment of this begins now in John 20 as the resurrected Jesus breathes the Holy Spirit into his disciples. *This is not a one-off event but an ongoing happening.* Are we to imagine that Jesus stops breathing the Spirit into those he lives with and in? Of course not. And it is striking that, in John's accounts of the resurrected Jesus, he comes freely *eis to meson*, into the centre of groups (20:19, 26), but there is never any mention of him leaving. *The visible who-to-who meetings are signs of the invisible, lasting who-to-who relationship.*

It is also striking that it is only now, at the end of this meeting with his disciples, that Jesus speaks of forgiveness. One disciple had denied him, and others had abandoned him. Now, he has greeted them with 'peace' and even gives them authority to forgive others: 'If you forgive the sins of any, they are forgiven them' (20:23).[5] It is as if it is only through receiving the peace and joy of the presence of Jesus, and after being energised for a future vocation and mission inspired by him, that we can face our own past and the past of others and be fully liberated from whatever has been wrong through receiving forgiveness.

'My Lord and my God!'

The third who-to-who encounter with Jesus is both with the group of disciples and focused on one individual: Thomas. It is pivotal.

It marks the vital transition from those who were eyewitnesses of the crucified and resurrected Jesus to us who were not. They experienced the actuality of the physical, visible presence of Jesus. The emphasis on this reaches its climax in his meeting with Thomas, who has doubted that the crucified, dead Jesus really is alive, and has asked for proof.

Jesus gives it: 'Then he said to Thomas, "Put your finger here and see my hands. Reach out your hand and put it in my side. Do not doubt but believe [and trust]"' (20:27). Thomas immediately does believe and trust, and responds with the culminating theological statement of the Gospel, crying out who Jesus is: 'My Lord and my God!' (20:28). *He has met with God.*

'Blessed are those who have not seen'

But then comes the pivot: 'Jesus said to him, "Have you believed, trusted, and had faith because you have seen me? Blessed are those who have not seen and yet have come to believe [trust and have faith.]"' (20:29). As John immediately makes clear (20:30–31), this is about us readers. We are the ones being blessed by Jesus. We have not seen Jesus, but the testimony to Jesus being given by John can either be trusted or not. *If we risk trusting it, and therefore trusting Jesus, we will be blessed. We too can meet with God.*

Mary has already been told by Jesus not to hold on to him physically because something better is about to happen – Jesus ascending to be present as God is present, intimately, permanently and lovingly, as anticipated in his prayer in John 17.

Thomas has just cried out the astonishing, core truth of who Jesus is – a visible human being who is also God. Once again, Jesus points to something more and better. Thomas's occasional, visible seeing is relativised. That is not the climax of relating to Jesus. If Jesus is indeed who Thomas says, 'Lord' and 'God', then he is free to be present as God is present – invisible, available to all who come to trust him and a permanent blessing.

At once, John addresses us readers:

> Now Jesus did many other signs in the presence of his disciples, which are not written in this book. But these are written so that you may come to believe [and trust] that Jesus is the Messiah, the Son of God, and that through believing and trusting you may have life in his name.
> (John 20:30–31)

The introduction to this book began with that passage because it is so important for us readers (and at this point it is worth rereading the introduction). John is not alone in giving reliable testimony to Jesus, but he has two particular purposes in his book. The first purpose is that readers may come to believe and trust in Jesus. As Thomas found, to meet, believe, trust and have faith in the crucified and resurrected Jesus is to meet God. The second purpose is that readers, through believing, trusting and having faith, may have life in his name. Having met God through believing, trusting and having faith in Jesus, we are to continue in permanent relationship with him – indeed, an eternal relationship of deep and lasting trust, life, love and glory. This ongoing relationship is what the rest of this book is about. But, before we move into that, there are two crowning thoughts about John 20.

How can we receive the Holy Spirit today?

The first is about receiving the Holy Spirit today. Jesus is utterly free to breathe the Holy Spirit into whomever he chooses. The language used for the Spirit in the Bible – breath, wind, water, fire – should make us wary of trying to tie the Spirit down, making it neatly containable or predictable or definable or controllable. Down the centuries, and around the world in our times, there has been a great deal of controversy about the Holy Spirit.[6] I think that the divisiveness of the disagreements could have been lessened – even avoided – by paying more attention to the Gospel of John. What can be learned from this Gospel about receiving the Holy Spirit today?

There are many lessons, but I will focus here on just one that stands out in John 20. The Holy Spirit is inseparable from who Jesus is and from the words of Jesus. So receiving and trusting Jesus as the Word of God, filled with the Spirit, and receiving and trusting his words as bearers of the Spirit are, for John, the main way to receive the Spirit. We have quoted some of the ways he prepares readers to understand this, such as 'He whom God has sent speaks the words of God, for he gives the Spirit without measure' (3:34), which is re-affirmed by what he says in his teaching after feeding the five thousand: 'The words that I have spoken to you are Spirit and life' (6:63). *Really to take in these words of life is to receive the Spirit.*

So the practical question is, 'How can we truly take in these Spirit-soaked words of life and the Spirit with them?' How can 'you abide in me, and my words abide in you'? (15:7). There is an obvious, straightforward way: *to read and reread and reread*, so allowing the words to inhabit us and us to inhabit the words.

For those who cannot read, and for those who can, this can be done by being read to, by hearing and listening and by learning by heart. Among the two billion or so Christians around the world today, it might be that the most common way of encountering John's writing is through hearing it in worship services or (directly or indirectly) through sermons, prayers, hymns, songs, liturgies, teachings and (perhaps most impactful) the lives and communities that this Gospel has helped to inspire.

The Spirit can, of course, work in many ways besides this, but anyone who seriously wants to receive the Holy Spirit from Jesus today would be foolish to ignore this core, basic way taught by John. *The Word* (both in person – Jesus the Word of God – and communicated through words, both in testimonies and in his own words) *and the Holy Spirit are inseparable.* The breath of Jesus carries his words and he himself, in all his words and actions, is the Word of God on whom the Spirit rests. And here in John 20, when we read of Jesus breathing the Holy Spirit into his disciples for the first time, it would be especially foolish to ignore the words he has just said: 'As the Father has sent me, so I send you' (20:21). It is as we take those words to heart, both personally and in our life together, and let them inspire our discipleship that we will experience the truth that 'The words that I have spoken to you are Spirit and life' (6:63). *Trusting those words, and trusting their speaker, the Word of God in person, is the straightforward way to receive the Holy Spirit and experience the abundance of life, truth, love and glory that Jesus desires for us.* How that can go on happening is the concern of the rest of this book.

Who is God?

The resurrection of Jesus is a God-sized event – as Thomas's cry, 'My Lord and my God!' (20:28), testifies.

The only adequate parallel is the creation of the universe. *As God is free to create out of nothing, so God is free to resurrect Jesus from death.* Paul talks of a 'new creation' (2 Corinthians 5:17), and here in John 20, the new beginning is with a man and a woman in a garden. The Prologue of John opens up this horizon of God, Jesus and creation right from the start, beginning with the opening words of Genesis: '*In the beginning* was the Word, and the Word was with God, and the Word was God … All things came into being through him, and without him not one thing came into being' (John 1:1–3).

The resurrection is not only the free action of God; its content is God. *God acts and Jesus appears.* Just as with the death and resurrection of Jesus and the giving of the Holy Spirit, John has prepared readers for this since the Prologue. In the chapters that follow, Jesus and his Father are utterly one, as seen especially in the 'I am' sayings of Jesus and the repeated insistence that the Father has sent him. The Father sending Jesus has its culmination in the resurrection of Jesus.

But even that is not all. That sending of Jesus has its culmination in the giving of the Holy Spirit. *God acts, Jesus appears and the Holy Spirit is given.* That is the full happening of the 'hour'.

This is who God is, as revealed over time through events. The way I have described it makes clear how John's Gospel has probably been the single most important text in identifying God as Father, Son and Holy Spirit; God as one in three and three in one; the Triune God; the Trinity. *Meeting this God involves meeting the invisible One, the Father who is the creator and sustainer of all that is, visible and invisible, and present to all that is;* meeting the One, Jesus Christ, who has freely come to us in full self-giving truth and love; and meeting the One, the Holy Spirit, who is the actual gift of the dynamic life and love of God in our living, learning, praying and loving, always drawing us deeper and further into glorifying God and following Jesus.

The next chapter explores what that life and following might be like in practice today.

Questions for individual reflection and group discussion

Suggested by Revd Canon Amiel Osmaston.

1 The risen Jesus asks Mary Magdalene who she is looking for in the garden (John 20:15). Who are *we* looking for? Are we expecting to meet the real, living Jesus who is shown to us in John's Gospel?

2 Jesus says twice to the fearful disciples as he appears to them in the upper room, 'Peace be with you' (20:19, 21). In what aspects of our own lives (and the lives of our community, nation and world) do we most need to receive Jesus' peace? How can we do that?

3 Jesus 'breathed on them and said to them, "Receive the Holy Spirit"' (20:22). Do we truly believe that we receive Jesus' Spirit?

How do we go on receiving, and what difference does this make to our lives?

4 Jesus says, 'Blessed are those who have not seen [me] and yet have come to believe [or trust, or have faith]' (20:29). How did Jesus lead you to believe and trust in him? Why do you continue to believe and trust in him?

Part 3

THE ONGOING DRAMA: JESUS HAPPENING IN THE TWENTY-FIRST CENTURY

We have seen in the Prologue of John's Gospel what *three essentials of a Christian worldview* are: God as the creator of all things and people, and the source of deep, superabundant meaning of many sorts; the deep, superabundant love of God, whose being is love; and, centrally, Jesus, who is one with God and one with us, who unites the deepest meaning and the deepest love, and invites us to share in his life, truth, and love. That was chapter 1 of this book.

We have also opened up *three essential questions* for disciples as learners, first raised in John 1: Who are you, Jesus? – the question of his identity, which leads into the question of our own identity; What are you looking for? – the question of what we desire, leading into how our desires can be educated and oriented, and, above all, who we desire; and, Where are you staying? – the question of home, which leads into the question of where we are most deeply rooted and permanently committed. That was chapters 2–4 of this book.

They all came together in chapter 5 of this book, on *the ultimate essential*: 'Glory – Meeting God in John'. To meet God through the Gospel of John is to meet in Jesus the glory of God, who unites the deepest meaning and the deepest love. This glory, truth, and love are encountered in who Jesus is, in what he does, and finally in 'the hour' of his crucifixion, his resurrection, and his gift of the Holy Spirit. The preparation for that climax – for Good Friday and Easter Sunday – culminates in the Last Supper, and especially in the prayer of Jesus in John 17. That astonishing prayer invites us into desiring the desire of Jesus for ourselves, for all humanity, and for all creation. His desire is for nothing less than for us to be united in glory, truth, and love with him and his Father, and with each other, for the sake of the world God loves. 'The glory that you have given me I have given them, so that they may be one, as we are one, I in them and you in me, that they may become completely one, so that the world may know that you have sent me, and have loved them even as you have loved me' (17:22–23).

Then we moved into the *three dramatic, essential happenings* of 'the hour': the Last Supper leading into the crucifixion of Jesus; the resurrection of Jesus; and the disciples receiving the Holy Spirit from Jesus. That was chapters 6–8 of this book.

The next chapter, after following the beginnings of life with the resurrected Jesus in John 21, goes back to the wisdom about discipleship in the Farewell Discourses to ask: what are the *essential practices* by which we who follow the crucified and resurrected Jesus are invited to shape our lives?

Finally, the Conclusion takes, as our guide into the future, the vocation and mission that Jesus gives his followers. He prayed to his Father for them in John 17, 'As you have sent me into the world, so I have sent them into the world'. Then, meeting with them after his crucifixion and resurrection, when he breathed the Holy Spirit into them he said, 'As the Father has sent me, so I send you' (20:21). What does this mean for us in the twenty-first century?

9

Christian essentials now: Jesus and learning, praying, loving

Read John 21.

'Simon Peter said to them, "I am going fishing." They said to him, "We will go with you"' (21:3). After the surprise of meeting the crucified and resurrected Jesus, these disciples get on with ordinary life and go back to fishing. But there is a series of new surprises. Jesus 'showed himself' (21:1; Greek *ephanerōsen*, which does not necessarily involve seeing) in a number of ways. Post-resurrection living is different.

Life with the resurrected Jesus: The 'extraordinary ordinary'

First, before they recognise who he is (showing that the resurrected Jesus can act anonymously), he helps them to catch a surprising number of 'large fish, a hundred and fifty-three of them' (21:11). It is yet another of the 'signs' of abundance that have happened time after time through the Gospel, such as the gallons of wine at the wedding in Cana (2:1–11), bread and fish for five thousand people (6:1–14) and, yet to come in this chapter, the final picture of so many books testifying to Jesus that 'the world itself could not contain' them (21:25).

The happening in an ordinary work setting is followed by an invitation to an ordinary meal: 'Jesus said to them, "Come and have breakfast."' Yet the disciples realise how extraordinary this meal is: 'Now none of the disciples dared to ask him, "Who are you?" because they knew it was the Lord' (21:12). The central question of the Gospel, 'Who are you?', is being answered in a way that makes it rash even to raise it. In Greek, 'it was the Lord' is *ho kurios estin*, literally meaning 'the Lord is'. This points to the central affirmation by Jesus of who he is in this Gospel: the divine 'I am'. Exactly the same words had just been used by the Beloved Disciple when he recognised Jesus, translated, 'It is the Lord!' and then immediately repeated by the author, translated, 'It was the Lord' (21:7).

The resurrection is about this new, permanent presence of Jesus, the divine 'I am', 'the Lord is'. Jesus the Lord simply is, whether he is seen or not.

Here, he is visible. 'Jesus came and took the bread and gave it to them, and did the same with the fish' (21:13). What is happening here has unmistakable echoes of Jesus feeding the five thousand with bread and fish (6:11). That led into extraordinary teaching (6:25–71). Rereading it now illuminates this breakfast and resonates beyond it with the ongoing Eucharist: 'This is the work of God, that you believe in him whom he has sent … I am the bread of life … The bread that I will give for the life of the world is my flesh … Those who eat my flesh and drink my blood have eternal life, and I will raise them up on the last day … Those who eat my flesh and drink my blood abide in me and I in them' (John 6:29, 35, 41, 54, 56).

But Jesus does not have to be visible for all this to happen: 'Blessed are those who have not seen and yet have come to believe' (20:29). It is as if John 21 is easing us readers into that time of blessing, our own time, a time of believing and trusting Jesus without seeing him and celebrating the presence of Jesus, his 'I am', in our shared meals. The third use of the verb *ephanerōsen* (21:14), meaning a 'showing' that can be either visible or not, also suggests this transition.

After these two signs of the 'extraordinary ordinary' experience of abundant life with the resurrected Jesus come two profound exchanges between Jesus and Peter, one centred on Peter himself and the other on the Beloved Disciple. Each exchange has the same culminating command: 'Follow me!' (21:19, 22). These are pointers to post-resurrection discipleship, to what matters most in the ongoing drama of following Jesus. And there is no doubt what matters most: *Jesus and love.*

Jesus, Peter and love (21:15–19)

'No one has greater love than this, to lay down one's life for one's friends' (15:13). Jesus has done this, but Peter has let him down. Can this friendship be renewed? Can there be a fresh start between Jesus and Peter? Can there be the two-way, freely given trust and love that are at the heart of what Jesus wants? We have considered this meeting before in chapter 3, but it is worth going deeper into it.

The first exchange with Peter signals a fresh start, as Jesus repeatedly reaches back to Peter's birth identity before he was called Peter by Jesus: 'Simon son of John' (21:15, 16, 17). With exquisite tact, there is no reference to Peter's denial of Jesus. Jesus simply asks, again and again, about what is utterly essential for the future: the love between them. 'Do you love me?' (21:16, 17). Each of us, day by day, is given this invitation to a fresh start in being loved and loving.

In response, Peter repeatedly commits himself in love. And it is a love that is united with being known through and through. 'Yes, Lord, you know that I love you … Lord, you know everything. You know that I love you' (21:15–17).

In response to that, Jesus sends Peter to love as he himself has loved: 'Feed my lambs … Tend my sheep … Feed my sheep' (21:16–17). Peter is to take part in nourishing a community of love inspired by who Jesus is as the good shepherd, as seen in John 10:1–39. That shows how he himself relates to 'my sheep' – calling each by name; enabling them to 'have life, and have it abundantly' (10:10); gathering others into 'one flock' with 'one shepherd' (10:16); and dedicated to this unity in love. The deep spring of all this is the love between Jesus and his Father: 'the Father loves me' (10:17); 'The Father and I are one' (10:30); 'the Father is in me and I am in the Father' (10:38).

And there is more, as will emerge from our study of the Farewell Discourses below.

Jesus also has more to tell Peter now, beginning with the emphatic, 'Very truly, I tell you' (21:18). As he had often indicated earlier, and in John 10 repeatedly, this is costly love: 'The good shepherd lays down his life for the sheep' (10:11); 'I lay down my life for the sheep' (10:15); 'For this reason the Father loves me, because I lay down my life' (10:17). Now this is to be learned by Peter, and at its heart it is a lesson about desire. When younger, 'you used to … go wherever you wished'. But, when old, 'someone else will fasten a belt around you and take you where you do not wish to go' (21:18). *To desire to love and follow Jesus is to find that some of our other desires have to be given up.* And one of those might even be our desire to avoid suffering and death: 'He said this to indicate the kind of death by which he would glorify God' (21:19).

Jesus, the Beloved Disciple and the future (21:20–24)

When he tells of Peter asking about the Beloved Disciple, the author pointedly recalls that 'he was the one who had reclined next to [Greek *epi to stēthos*, meaning 'on the breast of'] Jesus at the supper and had said, "Lord, who is it that is going to betray you?"' (21:20). That vividly pictures the profound contrast between, on the one hand, the anonymous disciple who is only known in this Gospel as 'the disciple whom Jesus loved' and who at that meal lay on Jesus' breast and, on the other hand, Judas who betrays the love of Jesus. That supper was also the occasion when Peter vowed to Jesus, 'I will lay down my life for you', but Jesus predicted, 'Very truly, I tell you, before the cock crows, you will have denied me three times' (13:37–38).

The sequel to that drama of love's betrayal and denial has just happened for Peter. Now comes the sequel centred on the Beloved Disciple. It has the three culminating surprises of this Gospel.

First, on the future of the Beloved Disciple and in response to

Peter's question, 'Lord, what about him?' (21:21), Jesus says, 'If it is my will [and desire] that he remain until I come, what is that to you? Follow me!' In the next verse, the author emphatically repeats the first part of it to counter a misunderstanding of it in the Church. That is a fascinating, multilayered statement.

- The statement continues and completes the theme of desire, which has run all through this Gospel. The Greek for 'will' is *thelō*, which also means 'desire'.[1] But now the focus is on the will and desire of Jesus. It is taken for granted that what he desires is primary. This is the final word on desire, which was the subject of chapter 3 of this book.

- The verb here translated 'remain' is *menein*, which also means 'to abide', 'to dwell' or 'to make one's home', and it was central to chapter 4 of this book. Where was the Beloved Disciple's home? We do not know, but what happened at the crucifixion tells readers with whom to imagine him living – the mother of Jesus: 'the disciple took her into his own home' (19:27).

- 'In the beginning was the Word, and the Word was with God, and the Word was God … All things came into being through him' (1:1–3). The Gospel opened with Jesus at the beginning of all created reality. Now, the Gospel ends with Jesus central to the future: 'until I come' (21:22, 23). The New Testament has some vivid scenarios for the return of Jesus, but the Gospel of John cuts through them to go for the core essential in all of them: Jesus. So the most important question about the future is not a 'what' question, such as Peter has just put to Jesus, or questions about when or how, but a 'who' question. Jesus is the central reality of the future. Of course! It is slipped in here as if it is simply taken for granted – and so it can be, if Thomas's cry, 'My Lord and my God!' (20:28) is taken seriously. The future is God's. Peter is told that he does not need to know the 'what' of someone else's future

– 'What is that to you?' (21:22). The essential is to trust that 'I come'. His future is to be centred on Jesus.

The way into that future is someone who is always present, the 'me' of the 'I am', the 'Follow me!' The next section will explore further what that involves.

But that exchange with Peter about the Beloved Disciple is only the first surprise at the culmination of this Gospel. The second is the revelation of the Beloved Disciple as the author of this Gospel: 'This is the disciple who is testifying to these things and has written them, and we know that his testimony is true' (21:24).

There are puzzles here. Who is the Beloved Disciple? Who are 'we'? And the next verse's 'I suppose' adds another anonymous person (21:25). There seems to be eyewitness testimony together with some involvement by the community of the Beloved Disciple. Scholars and others continue to ponder these puzzles.

What rings true to me (and what I think is in line with the mainstream of Christian tradition down the centuries and around the world today) is something like this: a close and authoritative eyewitness follower of Jesus lives long enough to take into account many other oral and written testimonies (20:30; 21:25), to mature his understanding and to learn from the experience of problems and divisions in his own community (as seen in the three Letters of John). All this results in the masterpiece of distilled essentials and depths of meaning that this lovingly crafted text gives to readers. His work is then treasured and edited within his community by the 'we' and the 'I' of 21:24–25. And why not imagine him sharing a household, conversation (perhaps even to the point of some co-authorship) and prayer with the elderly mother of Jesus in the earlier years of that long process of going deeper and deeper into what it means to 'remain until I come' (21:11)?

Then comes the third, final surprise: 'But there are also many other things that Jesus did; if every one of them were written down,

I suppose that the world itself could not contain the books that would be written' (21:25).

That is a gloriously open ending! Those 'other things that Jesus did' did not stop happening after the things described in John's Gospel. They went on happening – because he went on happening – up to the moment those words were written, and it is not surprising that to write about them and describe them adequately would need books that would overflow the world.

And they still go on happening – because he still lives – so the books go on being written, including this one. Jesus goes on being the divine 'I am', the bread of life, the light of the world, the good shepherd, the resurrection and the life, the way, the truth and the life, Lord and Teacher, the Saviour of the world, the Son of God, the Son of Man, the Messiah, the Word and more. Jesus goes on loving, serving and knowing us, giving us living water, doing signs of abundant life for all, sharing glory, peace, truth and joy, breathing the Holy Spirit into us and more. He goes on asking us questions: What are you looking for? For whom are you looking? Where are you staying, abiding, truly at home? Do you love me? He goes on stretching our imaginations through images of wine, wind, water, bread and fish, light and darkness, scent, childbirth, blood, receiving, lifting up and many more. He goes on giving commands that are also invitations to do things that he knows will give us deep and lasting life and joy, encouraging us to find ways of following his example of foot-washing, loving as he has loved, and to being sent as he was sent. As the deep secret of all that, he invites us to abide in him as he abides in us. His ultimate desire is, as he prayed to his Father, 'that the love with which you have loved me may be in them, and I in them' (17:26).

How can we cope with being loved like that by Jesus? We need a course in discipleship, in learning to receive and give love, and that is one way of describing the Farewell Discourses to which we now turn.

Being disciples: Three essential practices

The basic, most essential thing about being a disciple is being loved. The model disciple is the Beloved Disciple, 'the disciple whom Jesus loved' (13:23; 19:26; 20:2; 21:7, 20). Making him anonymous underlines the essence of discipleship: he is known by being loved by Jesus.

Of course, it is not only his disciples who are loved by Jesus; the good news is that his love, which is the love of God, is for all. 'God so loved the world that he gave his only Son' (3:16). Jesus shows this in many ways – through healing, feeding, forgiving and other actions, through teaching and conversation, through gathering a community of friends and, above all, through suffering and dying: 'And I, when I am lifted up from the earth, will draw all people to myself' (12:32).

What is essential for someone to respond to Jesus by becoming a disciple? John (together with all the Gospels, Paul and the rest of the New Testament) is very clear: believing in Jesus, trusting in Jesus and having faith in Jesus – all of which, as we have seen throughout this book, are included in the Greek verb *pisteuein*. John makes it a headline in the Prologue: 'But to all who received him, who believed [trusted and had faith, (*pisteuousin*)] in his name, he gave power to become children of God' (1:12). The saying from 3:16 just quoted continues 'so that everyone who believes [trusts and has faith (*pisteuōn*)] in him may not perish but have everlasting life.' When he is asked, 'What must we do to perform the works of God?' Jesus answers, 'This is the work of God, that you believe [trust and have faith (*pisteuēte*)] in him whom he has sent' (6:28–29). And so on, time and again throughout the Gospel, culminating in addressing us readers to tell us the whole purpose of writing the Gospel: 'so that you may come to believe [trust and have faith (*pisteuēte*)] that Jesus is the Messiah, the Son of God, and that through believing [trusting and having faith (*pisteuontes*)] you may have life in his name' (20:31).

This makes deep sense in relation to the love of Jesus. Jesus does not want love to be one-way; he wants it to be mutual. But for this to happen, he has to be trusted, and his love has to be received in trust. He is utterly committed in love. We can only begin to respond adequately by first of all trusting him. That is the bottom line. Trusting who Jesus is means trusting that we are utterly loved. And the only suitable response to this love is love.

The Beloved Disciple models this:

- At the Last Supper, he is leaning on the breast of Jesus in complete mutuality.
- At the crucifixion, Jesus embraces him as his own family, as son of his own mother like Jesus himself, entrusting her to him and him to her. He responds by forming a new household with her. This is deep trust and love happening.
- On Easter Sunday, it is the Beloved Disciple who goes into the empty tomb, sees the linen wrappings that had been around Jesus' body, 'and believed [trusted and had faith (*episteusen*)]' (20:8). He is the first believer in the resurrection of Jesus, and he has believed without actually seeing the resurrected Jesus. He could even be seen as receiving in advance the blessing of Jesus on us who come later: 'Blessed are those who have not seen and yet have come to believe' (20:29).
- After the large catch of fish, he is the first to recognise Jesus: 'It is the Lord!' or 'The Lord is!' (21:7).
- Jesus then, as just discussed, describes him as remaining, or abiding, into the future. That recalls the fundamental description of ongoing discipleship in the parable of the vine, with the ultimate in loving mutuality: 'Abide in me as I abide in you ... As the Father has loved me, so I have loved you; abide in my love' (15:4–9).
- Finally, he is revealed as the author of this Gospel, fulfilling in an exemplary way the calling of a disciple to give testimony and to be a faithful, trustworthy witness.

The Beloved Disciple is the fullest embodiment of who and what matters most in discipleship: Jesus and love. We now turn especially to the Farewell Discourses for wisdom about what that might involve in ongoing discipleship.

Learning

As we saw earlier, disciple simply means 'learner', and in Jesus' first conversation with his first disciples they called him '"Rabbi" (which translated means Teacher)' (1:38). Just before that, in his first words to them, he had done what is essential to good teaching and asked them a question. It was a question that goes to the heart of learning: 'What are you looking for?' Then, immediately after calling him Teacher, they do what is essential to good learning and ask him a question: 'Where are you staying?' Note how he answers: 'Come and see' (1:39).

He does not first of all give them instruction, tell them a story, do a striking 'sign', set them an example or challenge them in some way. 'They came and saw where he was staying, and they remained with him that day' (1:39). He shared his home with them, a place where they could get to know him. We do not know what went on during those hours, but we see the main result immediately. They did get to know who he was – 'We have found the Messiah' (1:41) – and a community of learners began to form around him. Andrew brought his brother Simon to Jesus, who said to him, '"You are Simon son of John. You are to be called Cephas" (which is translated Peter)' (1:42). *This is a community in which what is most important is who Jesus is, who each person is and being together – sharing a home, being a family and living together.*

The community needs practices to sustain this life together. The Farewell Discourses are where Jesus, when he is alone with his disciples at the Last Supper, sums up his teaching about three life-shaping practices: *learning, praying and loving.* They are interwoven and inseparable, but it is helpful to consider them one by one.

Teaching, and therefore learning, covers all the Farewell Discourses: John 13, 14, 15, 16 and even the prayer of Jesus in chapter 17, which teaches prayer by example. Besides the teaching on praying and loving, which will be considered in the next two sections, there is also very important teaching about the sort of learning that discipleship involves. It is worth reading through John 13 – 17 asking about this. I offer four thoughts to bear in mind while doing this.

First, notice why learning and loving are completely interwoven. It is because of who Jesus is and what he does and says. The core learning in discipleship is learning to trust that we are loved and called to love by Jesus, who is 'the truth' in person (14:6). The headline action Jesus does at the beginning of the Last Supper is to lovingly wash the feet of his disciples and then insist that this is what they have to learn from him as their 'Lord and Teacher' (13:13–14). In chapter 6 of this book, we have gone deeper into this as a key teaching.

This emphasis on learning who Jesus is and what he does and says runs all through the Farewell Discourses and culminates in his final prayer. There, knowing Jesus is at the heart of deep, lasting life with God: 'And this is eternal life, that they may know you, the only true God, and Jesus Christ whom you have sent' (17:3). And he himself as the truth is at the heart of the vocation of his disciples: 'Sanctify them in the truth; your word is truth. As you have sent me into the world, so I have sent them into the world. And for their sakes I sanctify myself, so that they also may be sanctified in truth' (17:17–19).

Second, notice that the disciples are 'sanctified in truth' together, in the plural, as a community. In the introduction to this book, I said that one striking thing about the Gospel of John is how it is crafted to make it suited to beginners, the very experienced and everyone in between. It is like a river in which 'mice can paddle and elephants can swim'. John's Gospel is a community book that can introduce us to Jesus for the first time and also draw us deeper and deeper into its meaning and truth over time. It enables both meeting Jesus and maturing in our relationship with him. The Church is a community in which at any one time there are people at very different stages of their Christian life, so what their learning involves can differ greatly. There is no limit to the stretching of hearts, minds and imaginations, and each is invited to be led further and further into 'all the truth' (16:13). But there is no sense at all in which this makes some superior to others. The model is our Lord and Teacher who washed feet.

Another aspect of this is that the Church is a community in which learning abilities are variously distributed, just as they are in the rest of society. For this reason too, what learning involves can differ greatly from one person to another without any hint of superiority or inferiority. I have been helped to learn this in practice by being part of Lyn's House, a mixed ability community of friendship in Cambridge. Jesus had daring friendships across all sorts of differences, and often with those marginalised within his society. That has been an inspiration to form friendships across differences in learning ability in Cambridge, a place best known for being centred on those with high levels of learning and expertise in many fields. Being in a community centred on those with learning disabilities has been like a fulfilment of the extraordinary promise with which Jesus concludes his teaching about the meaning of his foot-washing: 'Very truly, I tell you, whoever receives one I send receives me; and whoever receives me receives him who sent me' (13:20).[2] A parallel saying of Jesus in the Gospel of Mark is also about true greatness, and is centred on a child, a quintessential beginning learner: 'Whoever welcomes one such child in my name welcomes me, and whoever welcomes me welcomes not me but the one who sent me' (Mark 9:37).

Third, notice how, all through the Farewell Discourses (and also through the rest of John and indeed all through the Bible), there is a special role for words. In John, this is intensified by the headline identification in the Prologue of Jesus as the Word of God in person. In the Farewell Discourses, the foot-washing leads on to the new commandment to love as Jesus has loved (John 13:34). Keeping the word of Jesus is vital: 'Those who love me will keep my word, and my Father will love them, and we will come to them and make our home with them' (14:23). The Holy Spirit – called the *paraklētos*, meaning 'advocate, helper, encourager, comforter' – is the Spirit of truth who 'will teach you everything, and remind you of all I have said to you ... he will take from what is mine and declare it to you' (14:26; 16:15). In the parable of the vine, we find the intensive integration of learning, praying and loving: 'If you abide in me, and my words abide in you, ask for whatever you wish, and it will be done for you ... As the Father has loved me, so I have loved you; abide in my love' (15:7–9).

Then, in his final prayer, Jesus interweaves learning, loving and praying in yet another way. He emphasises God's word and words: 'they have kept your word ... for the words that you gave to me I have given to them, and they have received them and know in truth that I came from you; and they have believed [or trusted or had faith] that you sent me ... and I speak these things in the world so that they may have my joy made complete in themselves ... Sanctify them in the truth; your word is truth' (17:6, 8, 13, 17). The desire of Jesus that his disciples become 'completely one' with himself and his Father, and with each other, is rooted and grounded in the love between himself and his Father, the love through which the world was created 'so that the world may know that you have sent me and have loved them even as you have loved me ... you loved me before the foundation of the world' (17:23–24). And all this is being communicated in an extraordinary prayer, which can be a model for ours.

Fourth, there is a simple, practical lesson that obviously follows from the importance of Jesus as the Word, and of the words of Jesus. We readers are being given the awesome possibility of receiving Jesus, together with his words that are 'spirit and life' (6:63), *through reading and rereading the words of this Gospel*. 'Blessed are those who have not seen and yet have come to believe [trust and have faith]' (20:29). As Ingrid Kitzberger rephrases that: 'Blessed are those who read and reread the Gospel and believe.'[3]

Praying

'But the hour is coming, and is now here, when the true worshippers will worship the Father in spirit and truth, for the Father seeks such as these to worship him' (4:23). Our worship, our prayer, is desired by God. Why? Because we are desired and loved by God. His desire, as seen in the Beloved Disciple and in the final conversation between Jesus and Peter, is for love to be as deep and as fully mutual as possible. Opening our hearts, minds and whole lives to God in trust and love through prayer is what God wants. *We can begin or re-begin this right now, whatever our situation; it is a way that leads ever further and wider and higher and deeper.* The prayer of Jesus himself in John 17, which has accompanied this whole book, is a measure of its dimensions. Through it, we are inspired to be open to more and more of the superabundant life of God – glory, joy, truth and love – as the astonishing reality of our ongoing life at home in God's family.

There is much more to be learned about prayer through John's Gospel, but for now I will note three fundamental truths.

First, *the central reality of prayer is who God is.* This is often signalled by focusing on the name of God. As we have seen in chapter 5 of this book, John's Gospel is utterly centred on God and God's glory, and the short exchange between Jesus and his Father, after Jesus announces the beginning of 'the hour', is immensely important:

> 'Now my soul is troubled. And what should I say – "Father, save me from this hour"? No, it is for this reason that I have come to this hour. Father, glorify your name.' Then a voice came from heaven, 'I have glorified it, and I will glorify it again.'
> (John 12:27–28)

That fullness and intensity of the divine life and love is perfectly mutual, and it can embrace us too:

I glorified you on earth by finishing the work that you gave me to do. So now, Father, glorify me in your own presence with the glory that I had in your presence before the world existed. I have made your name known to those whom you gave me from the world ... I made your name known to them, and I will make it known, so that the love with which you have loved me may be in them, and I in them.

(John 17:4–26)

That is the knowledge of God and love of God at the heart of our prayer.

Second, *such prayer is the depth and spring of our action*. The Farewell Discourses not only culminate in the prayer of Jesus; they also include waves of his teaching on prayer. Perhaps most extraordinary is this:

Very truly, I tell you, the one who believes [trusts and has faith (Greek *pisteuōn*)] in me will also do the works that I do and, in fact, will do greater works than these, because I am going to the Father. I will do whatever you ask in my name, so that the Father may be glorified in the Son. If in my name you ask me for anything, I will do it. If you love me, you will keep my commandments. And I will ask the Father, and he will give you another Advocate, to be with you for ever.

(John 14:12–16)

Praying in the name of Jesus – asking in line with who Jesus is, inspired by the desire of Jesus for God to be glorified and love to be practised – will, amazingly, lead us to do 'greater works' than Jesus during his ministry. The previous chapter's foot-washing already redefined 'greatness' if it is to be in line with who Jesus is as 'Teacher and Lord ... Lord and Teacher' (13:13, 14): it is humble service in love. So in prayer we are to discern what new and 'greater' humble loving service we are being inspired to do by Jesus and the Spirit he gives.

Third, *the horizon of our prayer, the divine ecology in which we play our part, is worship 'in spirit and in truth'.*

That is the 'truth' first opened up by the Prologue, with its horizon of God and all reality, all creation, all people, all religions, all cultures, all knowledge, all parts of ourselves and each minute of our lives. John's Gospel is soaked in the Psalms,[4] the great worship book of the Bible, and in appendix B to this book, I recommend a way of immersing ourselves daily in the Gospel of John in a form similar to that in which so many worshippers, down the centuries and around the world today, have been and continue to be immersed in the Psalms.

By worshipping 'in spirit/Spirit' we are opened up to the surprises of the Spirit of the living God, like a wind blowing where it wills (3:8). We are drawn deeper into the intimate abiding in trust and love that Jesus desires for us in the parable of the vine in John 15 and in his prayer in John 17. And in that abiding, we can receive the Holy Spirit being breathed into us minute by minute by the crucified, resurrected and ascended Jesus Christ.

Loving

We have already seen how the Farewell Discourses deeply and inseparably interweave learning and praying with loving. But they also make clear the embracing priority of loving – from the first verse, 'Having loved his own who were in the world, he loved them to the end' (13:1), to the last, 'so that the love with which you have loved me may be in them, and I in them' (17:26). In between come waves of teaching on love.

In chapter 6, 'Thursday: Loving utterly, intimately, vulnerably, mutually', we especially focused on Jesus washing the feet of his disciples. That was the action and example that led into him giving 'a new commandment, that you love one another. Just as I have loved you, you also should love one another. By this everyone will know that you are my disciples, if you have love for one another' (13:34–35). Judas, his betrayer, had his feet washed along with the others, and was fed by Jesus, loved by Jesus. There is no idealised view of the followers of Jesus in the New Testament, and certainly not in the Gospel of John; there is misunderstanding, foolishness, stealing, betrayal, denial, rumour-mongering and more. But there is also an utter confidence that such things need not have the last word. There has been a happening, centred in the person of Jesus and continuing to happen through him and the Spirit he gives, because of which such things have been overcome and can continue to be overcome.

If we want to be part of this ongoing happening, it is essential to commit ourselves to being part of this imperfect community and to be open-eyed about our own imperfections and those of our community. As the First Letter of John – which can be read as the first, profound commentary on the Gospel of John written to a Christian community facing serious problems and divisions – says, 'If we say that we have no sin, we deceive ourselves, and the truth is not in us. If we confess our sins, he who is faithful and just will forgive us our sins and cleanse us from all unrighteousness' (1 John 1:8–9).

That leads into an emphasis on the priority of Jesus and love as what matters most, an insistence that is, if anything, even more passionate and intense in this letter than in the Gospel. It is a letter that returns again and again to being loved, to loving and to mutual abiding. The climactic, embracing, repeated truth is that 'God is love':

Whoever does not love does not know God, for God is love. God's love was revealed among us in this way: God sent his only Son into the world so that we might live through him. In this is love, not that we loved God but that he loved us and sent his Son to be the atoning sacrifice for our sins. Beloved, since God loved us so much, we also ought to love one another ... By this we know that we abide in him and he in us, because he has

given us of his Spirit ... God is love, and those who abide in love
abide in God, and God abides in them.
(1 John 4:8–16)

But quotations are not enough. It is worth reading and rereading the
whole love-soaked letter now.

Back in the Gospel's Farewell Discourses, there is a further wave
of teaching on love which goes deeper into that happening. It goes
beyond the loving service of foot-washing and into the mutuality of
love and knowledge in friendship:

> This is my commandment, that you love one another as I
> have loved you. No one has greater love than this, to lay down
> one's life for one's friends. You are my friends if you do what I
> command you. I do not call you servants any longer, because
> the servant does not know what the master is doing; but I
> have called you friends, because I have made known to you
> everything that I have heard from my Father.
> (John 15:12–15)

*That connection of friendship with sacrificial love to the point of laying
down one's life sets up a permanently challenging invitation into deeper and fuller community life that is oriented, like the death of Jesus,
towards a world whose deepest need is for trust and love.*

There is yet one more wave, this time the massive breaker of glory, truth and love happening through the prayer that is John 17. It
has been part of this book since the beginning, connected with the
Lord's Prayer so as to suggest that, like the Lord's Prayer, it is worth
repeated and even daily engagement, opening ourselves to it so that
we inhabit it, and it inhabits us. Who could ever fathom it? Trying
to do so stretches us spiritually, intellectually, imaginatively and
practically – both personally and as communities. It combines radical intimacy with a horizon stretching back to before creation and

embracing the whole world now and in the future. It is the ultimate desire of Jesus as he prepares to lay down his life in love. *Do we really desire to share his desire for utter unity in love with him and his Father, and with each other in the community of his disciples, for the sake of the world God loves? Is this the vision and the reality that inspires our learning, praying and loving? Are we committed to being part of this love happening on earth as it does in heaven?*

Yet for us, as for Jesus, desire and commitment need to be followed through into action and, if necessary, suffering. Jesus in this prayer says to his Father, 'As you have sent me into the world, so I have sent them into the world' (17:18). The conclusion of this book asks what that might mean for us today.

I suggest praying again the Lord's Prayer in the light of John 17 before reading it.

Questions for individual reflection and group discussion

Suggested by Revd Canon Amiel Osmaston.

1 In John 21:15–20, Jesus takes away Peter's sense of guilty failure and offers him a fresh start in love. Jesus repeatedly asks, 'Do you love me?' Peter repeatedly affirms his love, and Jesus tells him, 'Feed my sheep' (21:17) and then, 'Follow me' (21:19). As we seek to be Jesus' disciples, what might these questions and commands mean to us now?

2 *Learning*: In this chapter, we read, 'The core learning in discipleship is learning to trust that we are loved and called to love by Jesus, who is "the truth" in person (14:6).' Do you agree, and if so, what are the implications?

3 *Praying*: Has this chapter (or any previous chapter) inspired you as to how we could open ourselves up more to the wonderful extent, depth and surprises of prayer? How?

4 *Loving*: Jesus gave us 'a new commandment, that you love one another. Just as I have loved you, you also should love one another. By this everyone will know that you are my disciples, if you have love for one another' (13:34–35). How can we keep loving in spite of the current failings or frustrations we see in people around us, as well as in God's Church and world?

Conclusion

Our future: Sent as Jesus was sent

'As the Father has sent me, so I send you' (John 20:21). That is a key guideline for followers of Jesus moving into the future. I have described it, in chapter 8 above, as giving us 'the triple thrust of Christian living'. Each thrust is typical of John's Gospel in this: it can begin right now, from wherever we are, and then it can go on maturing and deepening as we are drawn further and further into the multifaceted abundance into which the Gospel invites us. It has the double dynamic that has run through this book: meeting God through coming to trust Jesus and then having ongoing 'life in his name' (20:31) – abiding in his love, being part of his family and one of his friends, committed to following him in the drama of living.

Into God

One thrust is into the reality of the living God and the sending of Jesus by the Father – who Jesus is, his relationship with his Father and the Holy Spirit, how he has been sent and his desire for the future.

That, of course, means considering and reconsidering the whole story of Jesus, every chapter of the Gospel. In practice, it involves reading and rereading the Gospel (or listening to it again and again), asking at each point, 'How can we understand this?' and, 'How can we enter more deeply into this abundance?' If we are sent as Jesus was sent, then such questions become part of daily living. They are at the heart of our ongoing life as disciples.

Likewise, the questions Jesus asks become ours. As we look to the future, perhaps none are more essential than those that ask about our desires: 'What are you looking for?' (1:38), 'For whom are you looking?' (20:15). That looking with desire is fulfilled through seeing and participating in the life, glory, knowledge and love of God that Jesus desires for us:

> Father, I desire that those also, whom you have given me, may be with me where I am, to see my glory, which you have given me because you loved me before the foundation of the world. Righteous Father, the world does not know you, but I know you; and these know that you have sent me. I made your name known to them, and I will make it known, so that the love with which you have loved me may be in them, and I in them.
> (John 17:24–26)

The central concern of this book has been for readers to desire like that, to meet and know God and to be part of that ongoing, God-centred life.

Into community

The second thrust is into the community of the followers of Jesus.

The 'you' in 'I send you' is plural. We are sent with others. All through this book, just as all through the Gospel of John (and, of course, through the rest of the Bible and in the wisdom distilled during two millennia of church history) there are lessons in how to be part of this community. The culmination in John's Gospel is in the Farewell Discourses, as described in the previous chapter of this book. As disciples of Jesus, our way into the future is through learning, praying and loving.

Again, there is that familiar double dynamic of the beginning and the ongoing. We can begin to learn, pray and love today whatever our situation. But who among us ever comes to the end of learning, praying or loving?

Again, the prayer of Jesus in John 17 can inspire us. He pours out his passionate desire for the community of his disciples. His desire is nothing less than for us to share fully, intimately and for ever in the life, glory, truth and love of God. It is a life that which none more desirable could be conceived or imagined. Pray through John 17 again and again! Imagine and reimagine it! Think and rethink it! And take very seriously its practical consequences for participation in the Christian community.

We are to be as deeply committed in love to one another as we are to God. This should make it almost inconceivable to make any move towards dividing any community of those who believe, trust and have faith in Jesus.[1] It should make Christian unity a top priority for every Christian and every Christian family, friendship group, community, organisation, network and church. Our core desire should be to fulfil the desire of Jesus for his followers: to be utterly united in trust and love with himself and his Father and with one another for the sake of the world God loves.

> The glory that you have given me I have given them, so that they may be one as we are one, I in them and you in me, that they may become completely one, so that the world may know that you have sent me and have loved them even as you have loved me.
>
> (John 17:22–23)

Again, one practice that can nourish all three essential practices of learning, praying and loving is reading and rereading, hearing again and again the Gospel of John, together as well as alone. 'I ask not only on behalf of these, but also on behalf of those who will believe [trust and have faith] in me *through their word*, that they may all be one' (17:20–21). That 'word' includes the Gospel of John, its intertexts throughout the Bible and, of course, the living key to all of them – Jesus Christ, the Word of God in person, breathing his Spirit into the readers and hearers of his words.

Into the world

The third thrust is into the world. As Jesus says in his prayer, 'As you have sent me into the world, so I have sent them into the world' (17:18).

The Farewell Discourses not only give a wisdom about the gathering of the community and its essential practices of learning, praying and loving but they are also realistic about the world into which Jesus was sent and into which his disciples are being sent. Both are sent into what John calls darkness – whatever denies, rejects, distorts or undermines the light and love seen in Jesus. The realism begins with darkness in the community of disciples itself. It is above all in Judas, who is associated with 'the devil' or 'Satan' (13:2, 27; later called 'the ruler of this world' in 14:30; 16:11). When Judas left to betray Jesus, 'it was night' (13:30). The dynamics of evil are both within individuals who bear real responsibility and beyond them. They are seen, for example, in the political, military and religious forces of the world, with which Judas allies himself. And, within the community of chosen disciples, Peter too succumbs to the darkness by denying his relationship to Jesus.

So, as chapter 6 of this book discussed, there is a double realism: it is about individuals going wrong and also about systemic forces of evil beyond individuals. The community of disciples is by no means immune to these. But there is actually a triple realism: the third, decisive reality is Jesus. Immediately after Judas goes into the night, Jesus says, 'Now the Son of Man has been glorified, and God has been glorified in him. If God has been glorified in him, God will also glorify him in himself and will glorify him at once' (13:31–32). The Farewell Discourses prepare the disciples for the glory of God happening in an unexpected way 'now', in the climactic 'hour' of the suffering, crucifixion and resurrection of Jesus. In this hour, as part 2 of this book described, the full intensity of the darkness happens to Jesus, but Jesus – utterly one, in love, with God and with us – also happens to the darkness. The result is Jesus alive in a new way, having overcome suffering, sin, evil and death.

The Farewell Discourses teach the meaning of this event and what will flow from it. Their realism about 'the world' includes not only the betrayal by Judas in alliance with the religious and political powers but also the prediction that the disciples will, like Jesus, suffer hatred, exclusion and persecution to the point of death (15:18–25; 16:1–4). But the crucial truth is that these do not have the last word. 'Very truly, I tell you, you will weep and mourn, but the world will rejoice; you will have pain, but your pain will turn to joy' (16:20).

The repeated message is that Jesus is the victor: 'the ruler of this world is coming. He has no power over me; but I do as the Father has commanded me, so that the world may know that I love the Father … The hour is coming, indeed it has come, when you will be scattered each one to his home, and you will leave me alone. Yet I am not alone because the Father is with me. I have said this to you, so that in me you may have peace. In the world you face persecution. But take courage; I have conquered the world!' (14:30–31; 16:32–33).

The preparation is completed in the prayer of Jesus in John 17. Jesus opens up the depths of his relationship with his Father and pours out his desire for his disciples to enter into those depths of life, glory, truth and love. But this is not just for themselves; it is to be shared. Just as his sending was in love for the world so too is the sending of his disciples. They will be hated by the world, they need protection against it and they, like Jesus, do not belong to it (17:11–16). But the purpose of their unity, in trust and love, with Jesus and his Father and with one another, is to attract the world into that same trust and love 'so that the world may believe [trust and have faith] that you have sent me … so that the world may know that you have sent me and have loved them even as you have loved me' (17:21, 23).

In the following chapters, John 18 and 19, the world does its worst to Jesus. In chapter 7 of this book, we followed the way John describes the trial and crucifixion of Jesus so as to bring home the utter centrality of who Jesus is, his identification with truth and love and the who-centred happening of his crucifixion. Now in John 20 comes the sending of his disciples into the world 'as' Jesus was sent by his Father. What might that little word 'as' mean for his followers' involvement with the world now?

'As' and improvisation

'As' (Greek *hōs*, *hōsper* or *kathōs*) appears at pivotal moments in John's Gospel, and it can illuminate each of the three thrusts just mentioned.[2] We began to explore its post-resurrection importance in chapter 8 above. If we are sent 'as' Jesus was sent, then we need to learn from and be inspired by how Jesus was sent and stay true to who he is, but we also need to live fully where we are now, as a community in the twenty-first-century world. This requires continual discernment, fresh imagining and thinking, and wise, creative communication and action. Jesus deeply and daringly related to his time and place and to the people he lived among, and so must we today.

This can be compared to improvisation in music. If musicians are to improvise well, they need to know the music as well as possible and practise their instruments thoroughly. Likewise, disciples need to know the 'music' of the Gospel as well as possible and be practised in learning, praying and loving. And if musicians are improvising together – not just as soloists – they need to practise together, alert and sensitive to one another, in synergy. Likewise in discipleship, learning, praying and loving need to happen both in each person's life and together in community. Then, the musical equivalent of public performance can happen: lively engagement with the world of today into which we are sent. In breathing the Holy Spirit into his disciples and sending them as he was sent, Jesus initiated a new time of inspired improvisation that is still happening.

Improvisation cannot be scripted. If it is written down note by note in a score, it is not improvisation. Down the centuries, the Gospel of John has inspired a vast array of responses in various contexts. It continues to do so, and we can study these and learn from them. I tried to do so in preparing my commentary and this book. But there is no reliable script for the future. Each day, week and year is unique and can bring surprises, even shocks, of many sorts. Each reader and group of readers is in a different situation, facing their own issues. There are core guidelines in John – what I have called essentials. Above all, they relate to the first two thrusts, and they are immensely important. Without them, our engagement with the world is not true to Jesus and what he desires.

But in relation to the particular contexts in which we find ourselves today, John's capacious 'as' encourages continual improvisation in the Spirit. Beginning in the Prologue, John sets up a dynamic Christian worldview that encourages us to go deeper – not only into God and the Christian community but also deeper into the world today – stretching our minds, hearts, imaginations and practical capacities. We can look through Christian history and at churches around the world today and learn from them, but there is no substitute for our own learning from John, our own prayer and worship, and our own inspired love and service in our own settings.

Two closing suggestions

At the end of this book are some appendices.

In appendix A, I set out a suggestion for how to pray the Lord's Prayer in the light of John 17. I hope that those readers who act on that suggestion will find it a worthwhile practice, and that the repeated references to John 17 through this book will help to encourage and deepen it.

In appendix B, I offer another suggestion: to read a little of the Gospel of John daily.

In the introduction, I said that my main hope for this book is that 'it might inspire readers, and even whole groups, congregations and communities, to become habitual rereaders of the Gospel of John itself.' But how might this be done? One way is to follow the practice of an Anglican parish priest, Alan Ecclestone. In the introduction to his book, *The Scaffolding of Spirit*,[3] he writes:

> One purpose has shaped this book. It is a plea for learning to read the Gospel according to St John with the kind of attention that can best be described as praying it. In doing that, I believe, we come nearest to the mind and intention of its author. In that way we latch on to what he himself did. He wrote that others might join him. I hope to suggest some ways of setting about it ... Reading in this way is not foreign to Jewish and Christian traditions of prayer. In just such deliberate fashion Torah was studied and Psalms were recited from time immemorial. They will go on being used in that way for generations to come. My plea is for doing that kind of prayer-reading of the Fourth Gospel. It would be like turning it into a Christian Psalter. Such use of it is greatly needed and long overdue.

In line with this, Ecclestone recommends prayer-reading a short portion of John daily, and he gives an appendix (which is reproduced in appendix B of this book) dividing up John into ninety readings so that one can reread it every three months. Karin Voth Harman – my vicar in St Andrew's Church, Cherry Hinton on the outskirts of Cambridge and the author of the foreword to this book – introduced this to our parish during a 'Year of John'. I began following it then, and at the time of writing am in my eighth cycle. It is continually inspiring, challenging and surprising, but also just part of ordinary life.

Whether daily or less frequently, I hope that the readers of this book will find themselves reading John habitually. And, in line with John 20:28–31, may you be blessed both by meeting God through Jesus Christ and by finding him fulfilling what he said: 'I came that they may have life, and have it abundantly' (10:10).

Appendix A
Praying the Lord's Prayer in the light of John 17

The Lord's Prayer is the best-known Christian prayer. Many, including myself, pray it at least once a day. Down the centuries, many have also found that the Lord's Prayer is illuminated and deepened by praying it in the light of the prayer of Jesus in John 17. Having discovered this nearly twenty years ago, I have found that the illumination and deepening continues. John 17 is at the heart of meeting God through the Gospel of John, so it plays a central part in this book. Many chapters try to fathom its inexhaustible depths. I suggest that, as a practical exercise for Lent (or any other time), you pray the Lord's Prayer in the light of John 17 as part of your daily prayer.

In order to help you get started (and hoping that you will find, with me and many others, that the practice never stops enriching your relationship with God), I offer a few suggestions and leading questions using a modern version of the Lord's Prayer.

'Our Father in heaven'

John 17: 'Father, the hour has come; glorify your Son ... So now, Father, glorify me in your own presence with the glory that I had in your presence before the world existed ... Holy Father ... Righteous Father.'
'Our Father in heaven', who loves us, is trusted and known above all through Jesus as Son of God, a core concern of John's Gospel.[1]

Jesus is not mentioned in the Lord's Prayer; John 17 draws us into being children of 'Our Father' in the closest possible relationship to Jesus. Jesus teaches the Lord's Prayer to his disciples in Matthew

6:9–13; here, his own relationship in prayer to his Father is shared. No wonder it helps us to pray!

This glimpse of the eternal divine life in its glorious intensity and intimacy leads on, later in this prayer, into that life and glory being opened up, astonishingly, to us: 'The glory you have given me I have given them, so that they may be one as we are one.'

'Hallowed [hagiasthētō] be your name'

John 17: 'I have made your name known to those whom you gave me from the world … And for their sakes I sanctify [hagiazō] myself, so that they also may be sanctified in truth … I made your name known to them, and I will make it known, so that the love with which you have loved me may be in them, and I in them.'

Who God is, God's name, is made known through Jesus. Note that the same Greek verb is translated as 'hallowed' and 'sanctify'. Jesus is the truth and love of God in person, and he wants us to be fully part of his most important relationship of being loved and loving.

'Your kingdom come'

John 17: 'Since you have given him authority over all people, to give eternal life to all whom you have given him.'

Again, Jesus illuminates the Lord's Prayer, with the kingdom of God being understood through his 'authority over all people' and his power to give deep, lasting life to everyone. This prayer is the culmination of his Farewell Discourses, which began with him transforming dominant ideas of authority by doing the slaves' work of washing the feet of his disciples, and then later calling them not only servants but friends. The 'eternal life' of this 'kingdom' is about mutual service and love.

'Your will be done'

John 17: 'I glorified you on earth by finishing the work that you gave me to do … The words that you gave to me I have given to them … As you have sent me into the world, so I have sent them into the world … so that the world may know that you have sent me, and have loved them even as you have loved me … so that the love with which you have loved me may be in them, and I in them.'

God's will is love!

The work finished by Jesus was the work of love: 'Having loved his own who were in the world, he loved them to the end … "It is finished"' (John 13:1; 19:30). The words he gives us in his 'new commandment' are 'love one another' (13:34; 15:12). Jesus is sent in love for the world: 'God so loved the world that he gave his only Son' (3:16). The deep, eternal spring of our love is 'the love with which you have loved me'.

'On earth as in heaven'

John 17: 'As you, Father, are in me, and I am in you, may they also be in us … so that they may be one as we are one, I in them and you in me, that they may become completely one, so that the world may know that you have sent me and have loved them even as you have loved me … so that the love with which you have loved me may be in them, and I in them.'

This is God's glory, life and love happening 'on earth *as in* heaven'. This abiding, this mutual indwelling of us in utter unity and love with Jesus and the Father, and with each other, for the sake of the world God loves – this is the uniting of heaven and earth.

Who could ever fathom the meaning of 'as' or 'in' in either the Lord's Prayer or this prayer of Jesus? How is the Father 'in' the Son and the Son 'in' the Father? What sort of unity is this? Who could ever sound the depths of what it is for us to participate 'in' that union? How has the Father loved the Son? And how can we cope with being embraced utterly by that love, having Jesus Christ himself, and his love 'in' us?

'Give us today our daily bread'

John 17: 'I glorified you on earth by finishing the work that you gave me to do ... May they also be in us ... I in them ... I in them.'

There is no mention of bread in John 17, but readers of John will remember two earlier statements by Jesus. He said to his disciples, 'My food is to do the will of him who sent me and to complete his work' (4:34; 'finishing' in John 17 and 'complete' in John 4 are the same Greek verb). And after the feeding of the five thousand (so making clear his concern that people have literal 'daily bread'), he identifies himself as 'the bread of life ... the bread that came down from heaven ... the living bread that came down from heaven ...' (6:35, 41, 51). There is then a direct connection with John 17 when Jesus goes on to speak of mutual indwelling for the first time: 'Those who eat my flesh and drink my blood abide in me and I in them' (6:56).

Readers of John will also be used to Jesus using other imagery, besides bread, which is associated with the things necessary for daily life, such as water, breath and light. John 17 simply sums up what Jesus gives as 'eternal life' (verse 3), the deep, lasting life that is given by him on both sides of death and includes physical food. He feeds them after his resurrection too: 'Come and have breakfast!' (21:12).

'Forgive us our sins as we forgive those who sin against us'

John 17: 'Holy Father ... so that they may be one as we are one ... sanctify them in the truth ... that they may all be one ... that they may be one as we are one ... that they may become completely one ... Righteous Father.'

The Father, and Jesus in unity with him, are loving, holy, truthful and righteous. To be at one with them and with one another is completely unimaginable without us being forgiven for everything in us that falls short in love, holiness, truthfulness and righteousness (which includes both personal goodness and social justice). The mutuality of John 17 cries out for the mutuality of forgiveness. The little word 'as' is again vital.

When the resurrected Jesus later fulfils his prayer in John 17 by sending his disciples as his Father sent him and breathing the Holy Spirit into them, he at once insists on the importance of forgiveness (17:18; 20:21–23).

'Lead us not into temptation but deliver us from evil'

John 17: 'Holy Father, protect them in your name that you have given me … I protected them … I guarded them, and not one of them was lost except the son of destruction … I am not asking you to take them out of the world but I ask you to protect them from the evil one.'

Jesus is realistic about the dangers of temptation and the forces of evil, often summed up in John's Gospel as 'darkness'. He prayed this as he was about to suffer and die, betrayed, denied and abandoned by his own chosen followers and sent to his death by an alliance of religious, political and military authorities. He was sent by his Father into that darkness, and so are his followers – and the darkness is in ourselves and in the Church as well as in the world.

That dark note at the end of the Lord's Prayer resonates with what the resurrected Jesus says to Peter near the end of John's Gospel: '"When you grow old, you will stretch out your hands, and someone will fasten a belt around you and take you where you do not wish to go." (He said this to indicate the kind of death by which he would glorify God.) After this he said to him, "Follow me"' (21:18–19). That shows that being protected does not necessarily mean being protected from death. There are worse things than death, such as the betrayal of trust and love by Judas, 'the son of destruction'. There is nothing better than to live and, if necessary, to die glorifying the God of love.

'For the kingdom, the power, and the glory are yours, now and for ever'

John 17: 'Glorify ... authority ... eternal life ... I glorified you ... glorify me ... the glory that I had in your presence before the world was created ... I have been glorified in them ... to see my glory, which you have given me because you loved me before the foundation of the world.'

This ending is not in Matthew's version of the Lord's Prayer and was added later by the Church. But it could have been inspired by John 17, with notes of authority, eternity and glory.

Amen.

Appendix B
John every ninety days

Table 1: John every ninety days

Day 1	1:1–9	Day 31	7:10–24	Day 61	13:21–30
Day 2	1:10–13	Day 32	7:25–31	Day 62	13:31–38
Day 3	1:14–18	Day 33	7:32–39	Day 63	14:1–7
Day 4	1:19–28	Day 34	7:40–52	Day 64	14:8–14
Day 5	1:29–34	Day 35	8:1–11	Day 65	14:15–24
Day 6	1:35–42	Day 36	8:12–20	Day 66	14:25–31
Day 7	1:43–51	Day 37	8:21–30	Day 67	15:1–6
Day 8	2:1–12	Day 38	8:31–38	Day 68	15:7–17
Day 9	2:13–23	Day 39	8:39–45	Day 69	15:18–27
Day 10	3:1–10	Day 40	8:46–59	Day 70	16:1–15
Day 11	3:11–15	Day 41	9:1–12	Day 71	16:16–24
Day 12	3:16–21	Day 42	9:13–25	Day 72	16:25–33
Day 13	3:22–36	Day 43	9:26–34	Day 73	17:1–11a
Day 14	4:1–14	Day 44	9:35–41	Day 74	17:11b–19
Day 15	4:15–26	Day 45	10:1–10	Day 75	17:20–26
Day 16	4:27–42	Day 46	10:11–21	Day 76	18:1–14
Day 17	4:43–54	Day 47	10:22–42	Day 77	18:15–27
Day 18	5:1–18	Day 48	11:1–16	Day 78	18:28–40
Day 19	5:19–29	Day 49	11:17–27	Day 79	19:1–16a
Day 20	5:30–38	Day 50	11:28–37	Day 80	19:16b–30
Day 21	5:39–47	Day 51	11:38–44	Day 81	19:31–37
Day 22	6:1–15	Day 52	11:45–57	Day 82	19:38–42
Day 23	6:16–21	Day 53	12:1–8	Day 83	20:1–10

Source: Appendix to Alan Ecclestone, *The Scaffolding of Spirit: Reflections on the Gospel of John* (London: Darton, Longman & Todd, 1987).

Appendix C
Christian thinking 1918–2024

The list of chapter headings in the fourth edition of *Ford's The Modern Theologians* is given below in order to give some idea of the range of Christian thinking mentioned in chapter 1 of *Meeting God in John.* I was only a consultant to the editors.

Ford's The Modern Theologians: An Introduction to Christian Theology since 1918 (Oxford: Wiley, 2024) edited by Rachel Muers and Ashley Cocksworth with David F. Ford

Table of Contents

Part II
Ecclesial Contexts

Part III
Theological Movements

Appendix C

Part VI
Theology Between Faiths

Part VII
Theology Facing Contemporary Challenges

Appendix D
Christian unity: A sign of hope

Running through this whole book has been John 17 in which, on the night before his death, Jesus pours out in prayer his desire for his followers to live united in love with himself and his Father, and with one another, for the sake of the whole world. Looking at the Christian Church around the world in the light of the desire of Jesus, it is easy to be discouraged, not least by how comfortable Christians often seem to be with a situation of many divisions so radically opposed to the will of Jesus. But there are also many signs of hope.

One that I have been observing with great appreciation for over two decades is the practice of Receptive Ecumenism.[1] It is deeply rooted in the remarkable history of the twentieth-century Christian ecumenical movement, through which many Christian churches moved from confrontation to conversation and from conflict to collaboration – and in some cases to full unity. But Receptive Ecumenism has faced the limitations of that movement, and it has opened up a creative yet demanding way forward, one that is now being practised in many parts of the world. At its heart is the act of inviting each tradition to face its own difficulties, wounds, distortions, ills and needs, and to be open to learning and receiving from other traditions in order to become more deeply, faithfully and creatively Christian. The goal is nothing less than full 'reconciled diversity' in love and truth in line with the prayer of Jesus in John 17.

The most recent development, pioneered by the Centre for Catholic Studies in the University of Durham in collaboration with the Rose Castle Foundation in which I am a participant, is the practice of Christian Biblical Reasoning.[2] This gathers Christians in small groups to read the Bible together across their divisions and differences.

It seems astonishing that, so far, there has been no widely accessible, flexible, tested practice available to divided Christians who want to read the Bible together. We have been neglecting an activity that is foundational for virtually all Christians: reading our Scriptures. Christian Biblical Reasoning is an attempt to develop such a practice. I hope that the present book will be a resource and encouragement for those who take part in it in the future.

Further reading

The amount of literature on the Gospel of John is immense and growing. I have limited my selection to fewer than thirty of the books I have found most illuminating in a variety of ways. They are given in alphabetical order, with a note added to each about why it has been chosen. My commentary on John (also included below) gives a much fuller list.

Augustine, *Homilies on the Gospel of John 1–40* (New York: New City Press, 2009). Translated by Edmund Hill. Edited by Allan D. Fitzgerald. Augustine is a profound, deeply influential thinker who is steeped in John.

C. K. Barrett, *The Gospel according to St. John: An Introduction with Commentary and Notes on the Greek Text* 2nd ed. (London: SPCK, 1978). A classic modern commentary on John in Greek by a great scholar and preacher.

Richard Bauckham, *Gospel of Glory: Major Themes in Johannine Theology* (Grand Rapids: Baker Academic, 2015); *The Testimony of the Beloved Disciple: Narrative, History, and Theology in the Gospel of John* (Grand Rapids: Baker Academic, 2007). Two books by one of the finest living New Testament scholars, who is also a theologian.

Jo-Ann A. Brant, *John* (Paideia. Grand Rapids: Baker Academic, 2011). A good shorter commentary, especially on John's literary crafting.

Raymond E. Brown, *The Gospel According to John: Introduction, Translation, and Notes* 2 vols (Anchor Bible 29, 29A. New York: Doubleday, 1966, 1970). The major work of a leading Catholic interpreter of John.

Frederick Dale Bruner, *The Gospel of John: A Commentary* (Grand Rapids: Eerdmans, 2012). The best Evangelical commentary on John that I have read.

Paul Cefalu, *The Johannine Renaissance in Early Modern English Literature and Theology* (Oxford: Oxford University Press, 2017). This fascinating study made me think, 'Why not have a similar John-inspired renaissance today?'

Mary L. Coloe, *Dwelling in the Household of God: Johannine Ecclesiology and Spirituality* (Collegeville, MN: Liturgical Press, 2007). A deep Catholic engagement with John relevant to Christian living now.

Margaret Daly-Denton, *David in the Fourth Gospel: The Johannine Reception of the Psalms*. (Arbeiten zur Geschichte des antiken Judentums und des Urchristentums 47. Leiden: Brill, 2000). John is steeped in the Psalms, and this book takes us deeper into both; *John: An Earth Bible Commentary* (London: Bloomsbury T&T Clark, 2017). A model of superb scholarship and rich reflection, especially relevant to our environmental crisis today.

Alan Ecclestone, *The Scaffolding of Spirit: Reflections on the Gospel of St John* (London: Darton, Longman & Todd, 1987). My favourite short popular book on John, which has also inspired me to follow his suggestion of reading John every day (see Appendix B).

Ruth B. Edwards, *Discovering John: Content, Interpretation, Reception* 2nd ed. (Discovering Biblical Texts. London: SPCK, 2014). A balanced, scholarly introduction to John.

David F. Ford, *The Gospel of John: A Theological Commentary* (Grand Rapids: Baker Academic, 2021). No comment!

Thomas Gardner, *John in the Company of the Poets: The Gospel in Literary Imagination* (Waco: Baylor University Press, 2011). Deep and inspiring, drawing on some of the best poetry I have read.

Richard B. Hays, *Echoes of Scripture in the Gospels* (Waco: Baylor University Press, 2016). One of the greatest of recent American biblical scholars shows how important and illuminating the Old Testament is for John and the other three Gospels.

E. C. Hoskyns and F. N. Davey, *The Fourth Gospel* (London:

Faber & Faber, 1947). A rich interweaving of scholarship and theology, with depth.

Dorothy Lee, *Flesh and Glory: Symbolism, Gender and Theology in the Gospel of John* (New York: Crossroad, 2002). Imaginative and deep, uniting scholarship, theology and spirituality; *John* (Grand Rapids: Zondervan, 2025). The most recently published book on this list, and an excellent way to access the mature insights of a fine Anglican scholar and theologian.

Denise Levertov, *The Collected Poems of Denise Levertov* (New York: New Directions, 2013). Edited by Paul A. Lacey and Anne Dewey. My favourite twentieth-century Christian poet, Levertov's later poetry is soaked in John and Julian of Norwich.

Judith M. Lieu and Martinus de Boer, eds. *The Oxford Handbook of Johannine Studies* (Oxford: Oxford University Press, 2018). An excellent distillation of much of the best scholarship on John.

Andrew T. Lincoln, *The Gospel according to Saint John* (Black's New Testament Commentaries. Peabody, MA: Hendrickson, 2005). Fine, reliable scholarship, with theological sensitivity and well-argued conclusions; the commentary I have used most.

Francis J. Moloney, *The Gospel of John*. (Sacra Pagina. Collegeville, MN: Liturgical Press, 1998). It is always worth consulting this major Catholic scholar in Australia who has helped to form an influential school of John studies there.

Lesslie Newbigin, *The Light Has Come: An Exposition of the Fourth Gospel* (Edinburgh: Handsel, 1982). The distilled wisdom of one of the great, prophetic church leaders of the twentieth century.

Gail R. O'Day and Susan E. Hylen, *John* (Westminster Bible Companion. Louisville: Westminster John Knox, 2006). A really good short commentary by two outstanding scholars whose judgement I trust.

Micheal O'Siadhail, *The Five Quintets* (Waco: Baylor University Press, 2018). A powerful work – fine, accessible poetry covering the arts, economics, politics, the sciences, philosophy and theology in recent centuries. I see it as a twenty-first-century filling out of John's 'God and all things' worldview.

Adele Reinhartz, *Befriending the Beloved Disciple: A Jewish Reading of the Gospel of John* (New York: Continuum, 2001). It is vital for Christians to attend to Jewish understandings of John.

Rudolf Schnackenburg, *The Gospel according to St. John* 3 vols (Herder's Theological Commentary on the New Testament. London: Burns & Oates, 1980–82). Translated by Kevin Smyth. A massive, profound Catholic commentary on John's 'theological history writing', with many gems if you persevere.

Notes

Introduction

1 The Greek word *pisteuein* means 'to believe' but also 'to trust'. Susan Hylen, one of the leading scholars of John's Gospel today, once said to me, 'I tell my students that in our culture it is wise to translate the Greek verb *pisteuein* in the first instance as "trust" – that gets the core meaning of this multifaceted word best, and then you can join this with its other meanings, such as believe, have faith, have confidence, entrust something to someone, be committed and more.'

1 The big picture: Meaning, love, Jesus

1 *The Modern Theologians: An Introduction to Christian Theology since 1918*, 3rd edn, edited by David F. Ford and Rachel Muers (Oxford: Blackwell, 2005); 4th edn, to which I have been a consultant, *Ford's The Modern Theologians*, edited by Ashley Cocksworth and Rachel Muers (Oxford: Wiley Blackwell, 2023).

2 Sadly, the NRSV loses the image that is given in the Greek *en tō kolpō* and translates it 'who had reclined'. Other translations do better.

3 In her book in this series, *Meeting God in Matthew* (London: SPCK, 2022), Elaine Storkey does something similar with the Gospel of Matthew in ways that harmonise very well with the Gospel of John. Rowan Williams, in *Meeting God in Mark* (London: SPCK, 2014), takes a different approach but also resonates richly with John.

2 Identity: 'Who are you?'

1 'Water is found in jars at Cana; as a symbol of rebirth; for baptism by John, Jesus and the disciples; in a well in Samaria; in the Pool

of Bethzatha; in the "Sea of Galilee"; in the pool of Siloam; in a basin for washing the disciples' feet. Moreover, the significance of water "expands as the narrative unfolds", climaxing in the waters gushing from the crucified Jesus' pierced side, something phenomenal that the Evangelist makes such a point of recording (19:34–35).' See Margaret Daly-Denton, *John: An Earth Bible Commentary* (London: Bloomsbury T&T Clark, 2017), p. 89.

3 Desire: 'What are you looking for?'

1 Other angles on the drama of desire in this Gospel include: the crowd seeking Jesus (6:24) and later being swayed back and forth (12:12–19; 18:38–40, 19:15); the seeking of glory for God rather than for oneself as vital to ringing 'true' as a person (7:18); the clash of good and bad desires at a level beyond the individual (8:39–47); the Father, not Jesus himself, seeking the glory of Jesus (8:50); Jesus perplexing his opponents, telling them, 'You will search for me, but you will not find me; and where I am, you cannot come' (7:34, 36; see also 8:21–30), and later telling his disciples the same (13:33); the coming of Greeks who 'wish to see Jesus' (12:21); and the extraordinary promise, 'If you abide in me, and my words abide in you, ask for whatever you wish, and it will be done for you' (15:7). Some of these will figure in later chapters of this book.

2 Note that 'the first of his signs' (2:11) at the Cana wedding and the last one at the Bethany funeral (11:4, 40) are both closely associated with glory, which will be the focus of chapter 5, 'Glory: Meeting God in John'.

3 On this fascinating theme, see David F. Ford, *The Gospel of John: A Theological Commentary* (Grand Rapids: Baker Academic, 2021), pp. 102–4, 112–14.

4 Home: 'Where are you staying?'

1 See Ford, *The Gospel of John,* pp. 178–81 on why I see this event as so momentous.

2 Think too of what Jesus says in Matthew 12:46–50: 'While he was still speaking to the crowds, his mother and his brothers were standing outside, wanting to speak to him. Someone told him, "Look, your mother and your brothers are standing outside, wanting to speak to you." But to the one who had told him this, Jesus replied, "Who is my mother, and who are my brothers?" And pointing to his disciples, he said, "Here are my mother and my brothers! For whoever does the will of my Father in heaven is my brother and sister and mother."'

3 For more on this see Ford, *The Gospel of John,* pp. 217, 231–5.

4 This also begins to make sense of why the understanding of God as both One and Trinity has been so important for Christians: it is about the unity of mutual indwelling in love. For more on the Trinity in John, see Ford, *The Gospel of John,* pp. 8, 12, 15, 36, 51, 104, 282, 305.

5 Glory: Meeting God in John

1 This is not to be understood as saying that God is literally male. The language of father and son is first introduced in John 1:14: 'glory as of a father's only son'. That little word 'as' is very important in the Gospel of John, as later chapters in this book will show. It signals metaphor, imagery and analogy. When Janet Soskice asks the question, 'Can a feminist call God Father?', she answers with a resounding, 'Yes!' She then gives a fascinating account of how ideas of who God is and what a father is are transformed by the New Testament. Of course, many other names, metaphors, images and analogies are used by both Soskice and the Gospel of John. See Janet Soskice, *The Kindness of God: Metaphor, Gender, and Religious Language* (Oxford: Oxford University Press, 2007) chapter 4, 'Calling God "Father"'. See also Ford, *The Gospel of John: A Theological Commentary,* p. 37.

2 Richard Harries: 'Praise begins in recognising something good, then appreciating and admiring it. It takes us out of ourselves as

we focus on what is worthwhile in itself. Sometimes the good is so good we are astonished and lost for words. For those keen on tennis it happened when Roger Federer was at his peak. It felt a privilege to have lived at a time when he played. Other people will be able to draw examples from elsewhere, ballet or football, music or gymnastics.' From 'Thought for the Day' on Radio 4, undated quotation.

3 For more on the glory of the smile, connecting it (in all its ordinariness) with love, joy and delight, revelation, mutuality, grace and gift, parent-child relationships, gratuitousness and spontaneity, welcome and hospitality, encouragement, participation, Dante's *Divine Comedy* and the Trinity, see Ashley Cocksworth and David F. Ford, *Glorification and the Life of Faith* (Grand Rapids: Baker Academic, 2023), pp. 118–29.

4 The way the First Letter of John sums this up is in two key statements about God: 'God is light' (1 John 1:5) and 'God is love' (1 John 4:8, 16).

5 See also the parallels in Mark 22:34–35 and Luke 10:25–28.

6 St Augustine in *On Christian Teaching* says that any interpretation of the Scriptures that goes against love of God or love of neighbour is wrong.

7 For the full poem, each verse of which can be savoured like a glass of the best wine, see Richard Wilbur, *The Mind-Reader: New Poems* (New York: Harcourt Brace, 1976), p. 12, and also Ford, *The Gospel of John*, p. 69.

6 Thursday: Loving utterly, intimately, vulnerably, mutually

1 The other is 'Blessed are those who have not seen and yet have come to believe' (John 20:29).

2 For their Rule of Life, see https://www.stanselm.org.uk/wp-content/themes/vu-theme/assets/images/RuleofLifeBooklet.pdf. The Rule is deeply shaped by the Gospel of John in many ways, not least in making basic to their life the prayer of Jesus in John

17, about which it says, 'This prayer is the basis for our unity in the Community of St Anselm ... We humbly accept Jesus' prayer as our own hearts' desire.'

3 For more, see Ford, *The Gospel of John*, pp. 49, 88, 141, 143, 156–7, 259, 277, 293–4, 390.

4 For a fuller account of what follows, especially on the threefold realism, see David F. Ford, 'The Gospel of John' in *Companion to Suffering and the Problem of Evil*, edited by Matthias Grebe and Johannes Grössl (London: T&T Clark, 2023).

7 Friday: Jesus dies

1 The NRSV translates 1:3 'All things came into being through him, and without him not one thing came into being. What has come into being ...' The key Greek verb, *ginesthai*, here occurring three times in one verse and translated as 'came into being', occurs no fewer than nine times in the Prologue and is variously translated (for example, in the NRSV as 'came into being', 'became', 'came', 'there was', 'become', 'was'). Common to all the translations is a sense of significant happening. The scope of Jesus-related happening opened up by the Prologue is nothing less than God and all reality, and it includes the ongoing life of the family of those who trust and believe in him (1:12: 'to *become* [*genesthai*] children of God'). The relationship of Jesus to God and God's eternal time is underlined by the use of the verb *ginesthai* in what John the Baptist says about Jesus in 1:15: *emprosthen mou gegonen*; NRSV 'he *was* before me', literally meaning 'he happened before me' (cf. 1:30; 8:58; 17:5, 24). This 'happening' verb occurs all through John's Gospel and the rest of the New Testament. It also occurs throughout the Greek translation of Israel's Scriptures, the Septuagint (the scriptural text most quoted by the Greek-speaking authors of the New Testament), beginning with the creation account in Genesis 1, which lies behind the Prologue of John: '*Let there be* [*genēthētō*] light and *there was* [*egeneto*] light' (Genesis 1:3). The verb occurs

twenty-three times in Genesis 1. Its range of meaning includes 'happen', 'come into being', 'become', 'prove to be', 'arise', 'occur', 'take place', 'be born', 'produce' and 'originate'.

2 For more on the Lamb of God and on all the examples that follow (each of which will repay meditation), see Ford, *The Gospel of John* and other commentaries highlighted and listed on p. 445 of that volume.

3 On Jesus being 'lifted up', see also 8:28, where again Jesus as 'Son of Man' and Jesus in relation to God's 'I am' come together in his crucifixion, which can be seen to go to the heart of both his humanity and divinity. See also 12:32–33 later in this chapter.

4 See chapter 6 above, 'Thursday: Loving utterly, intimately, vulnerably, mutually'.

5 The Greek for 'completely one', *teteleiōmenoi eis hen* (17:21) connects directly with the language used about the death of Jesus, as in 'he loved them *to the end*', *eis telos* (13:1), and 'all was now *finished* … "It is finished"', '*tetelestai* … "*tetelestai*"' (19:28, 30), all sharing a common root pointing to finishing, completion, perfection and fulfilment.

6 Looking ahead to the appearance of the resurrected Jesus to Thomas (John 20:24–29), the cry of Thomas, 'My Lord and my God!' uses two titles that were also given to the Roman emperor – Latin *dominus* and *deus*. Christians in the Roman Empire were to die as martyrs rather than honour the emperor as divine.

7 Denise Levertov, *Breathing the Water* (New York: New Directions, 1987), pp. 68–9. For the complete poem and a fuller discussion of it, see Ford, *The Gospel of John*, pp. 381–4.

8 The Greek root *tel* in 'completely' is also in the words 'finished', 'fulfil' and 'finished' in 19:28, 30; in 'finishing' in 17:4; and in 'end' in 13:1.

8 Sunday: Jesus alive

1 I read the First Letter of John as the first response to and

commentary on the Gospel of John that we have. One striking
thing the letter does is to intensify and sum up some essentials
of the Gospel, such as the crucial importance of love in the
community and of the Spirit, truth and abiding in Jesus. Central to
all this is who Jesus is as 'the word of life' in person (1 John 1:1), the
Son of God who is at one with God who 'is light' (1 John 1:5) and
'is love' (1 John 4:8). Who Jesus is embodies the living God of truth
and love.

2 Analogies to this singular, God-sized event are bound to be
inadequate, but one I find helpful in suggesting the crucial
importance of the 'who' factor in a transformative event comes
from twentieth-century South Africa. There, apartheid happened
to Nelson Mandela, and he suffered decades of imprisonment
for opposing it. But Nelson Mandela also happened to apartheid.
It probably saved South Africa from a massive bloodbath that,
through those years in prison, Mandela became the sort of person
who could risk negotiating the end of apartheid with F. W. De
Klerk, and had the moral and political authority to envision South
Africa as a rainbow nation even though many of his supporters
thought that violence was the only realistic way. And then, out of
prison, he became the first post-apartheid president.

3 The Greek *humas*, meaning 'your', is plural.

4 The Greek word here translated as 'home' is *monē*, whose verb form
is *menein*, meaning 'abide', 'dwell', 'last', 'endure' and 'live in'. In
the parable of the vine in John 15, this is the key term to describe
the ongoing relationship of Jesus and his followers. In this book,
see especially chapter 4 'Home: "Where are you staying?"'

5 The second part of this verse has two very different possible
translations. See Ford, *The Gospel of John,* pp. 407–8 for a
discussion of them.

6 It is an ongoing tragedy in the history of the Church that, time
and again, Christians have been divided by conflict about the Holy
Spirit. The schism between the Eastern and Western churches

around the year 1000 was (officially) about the Holy Spirit. Central to the sixteenth-century Protestant Reformation's break with Catholicism was how to understand the grace of God, which is inseparable from how the Holy Spirit is understood. And, in the twentieth century, Pentecostalism, the largest ever Christian revival movement, now embracing hundreds of millions of people worldwide, found that its understanding and experience of the Holy Spirit could not be contained or done justice to by existing churches.

9 Christian essentials now: Jesus and learning, praying, loving

1 The same Greek word is translated 'wished … wish' in 21:18 above about Peter.

2 See David F. Ford, Deborah Hardy Ford and Ian Randall (eds), *A Kind of Upside-downness: Learning Disability and Transformational Community*.

3 Quoted by Margaret Daly-Denton in support of her own conclusion about John's Gospel, 'This is a text that calls for re, re, and re-readers', in *John: An Earth Bible Commentary*, p. 10.

4 Margaret Daly-Denton does a superb study of this in *David in the Fourth Gospel: The Johannine Reception of the Psalms* (Leiden: Brill, 2000).

Conclusion

1 I completely agree with those scholars who see the massive emphasis in John's Gospel on unity in love among disciples of Jesus being partly due to the experience of disunity in the early church. The Letters of John in the New Testament show that the community most associated with the Gospel of John was itself experiencing conflict and division. What I have described as the Christian essentials are John's distillation of what should unite Christians. The other side of this is a major challenge to almost

every Christian community today: be very, very, very reluctant ever to divide from fellow Christians (defined as those who believe, trust and have faith in Jesus in line with the Gospel of John) on the basis of anything not in the Gospel of John. The First Letter of John in particular shows these essentials being mobilised in support of a united community. It is also striking that just as John, most likely the final Gospel to be written, inspires this passionate commitment to Christian unity in love, so the Letter to the Ephesians, which represents matured theology in the tradition of Paul (scholars differ about whether it was actually written by Paul) has exactly the same emphasis. It is summed up in a passionate appeal: 'I, therefore, the prisoner of the Lord, beg you to lead a life worthy of the calling to which you have been called, with all humility and gentleness, with patience, bearing with one another in love, making every effort to maintain the unity of the Spirit in the bond of peace. There is one body and one Spirit, just as you were called to the one hope of your calling, one Lord, one faith, one baptism, one God and Father of all, who is above all and through all and in all' (Ephesians 4:1–6). The extraordinary prayer at the centre of the letter (Ephesians 3:14–21), which leads into this passage, has deep resonances with both the Lord's Prayer and John 17. All three are well worth including as part of our daily prayer. Yet to pray them also intensifies the anguish and agony of experiencing the ways in which we Christians repeatedly violate them, resisting the desire of Jesus. As I look at the deeply divided Church around the world today, the sign of hope that I have found most encouraging is the practice of Receptive Ecumenism, as developed by Professor Paul Murray and the Centre for Catholic Studies in the University of Durham. Appendix D to this book says a little more about it.

2 See Ford, *The Gospel of John,* pp. 9, 13, 37, 94, 95, 201, 210, 260, 266, 295, 329, 330, 343, 344, 346, 404.

3 Alan Ecclestone, *The Scaffolding of the Spirit: Reflections on the Gospel of* John (London: Darton, Longman & Todd, 1987), p. 2.

Appendix A

1 To repeat the first note for chapter 5, this is not to be understood as saying that God is literally male.

Appendix D

1 The most easily accessible way to understand this is through the website of the Centre for Catholic Studies in the University of Durham, https://www.durham.ac.uk/research/institutes-and-centres/catholic-studies/research/constructive-catholic-theology-/receptive-ecumenism-/. There is now a large literature on Receptive Ecumenism, two of the major works being *Receptive Ecumenism and the Call to Catholic Learning: Exploring a Way for Contemporary Ecumenism* edited by Paul D. Murray (Oxford: Oxford University Press, 2008); and *Receptive Ecumenism as Transformative Ecclesial Learning. Walking the Way to a Church Re-formed* edited by Paul D. Murray, Gregory A. Ryan and Paul Lakeland (Oxford: Oxford University Press, 2022) to which I contributed a chapter: David F. Ford, 'Mature Ecumenism's Daring Future: Learning from the Gospel of John for the Twenty-First Century'.

2 See the Rose Castle Foundation website, https://www.rosecastlefoundation.org.

Index

175

Index

Index

The Big Church Read

Did you know that you can read

Meeting God in John

as a **Big Church Read?**

Join together with friends, your small group
or your whole church, or do it on your own, as
12 dynamic voices lead you through the book.

Visit www.thebigchurchread.co.uk or use the
QR code below to watch exclusive videos exploring
the ideas and themes of *Meeting God in John.*

The Big Church Read will also **provide you with a reading plan
and discussion questions** to help guide you through the book.

It's free to join in and a great way to read through
Meeting God in John!

www.ingramcontent.com/pod-product-compliance
Lightning Source LLC
La Vergne TN
LVHW052024080426
835513LV00018B/2142